Advance Praise About the Book

"I whole-heartedly recommend this book to anyone who aspires to be a published author. Its easy-to-read format is practical, focused, and helps turn a dream into reality."
✏ Patricia A. Perry, author of *The Haunting of the Owens Family*

"This book is a must have for anyone considering trying to become a published author!"
✏ Johnny May, author of *Johnny May's Guide to Preventing Identity Theft*

"If you want to write and publish a book, read this first. Bond's conversational style of writing makes it seem easy. And maybe it is."
✏ Greg Bussy, Marketing Manager, Oxford University Press

"Not too often can you find pertinent, informative instruction presented in such an enjoyable format. What a valuable read!"
✏ Joseph M. Celli, author of *First Aid for Home Sellers*

"You Can Write and Publish a Book *is a very well written book from a professional writer with an easy-to-use plan to assist in writing and publishing a book. An extremely valuable resource."*
✏ Dr. Robert A. Gray, Chair, Library Science and Instructional Technology Department, Kutztown University, Kutztown, Pennsylvania

"Got a book in you? For the pep talk you need to make it a reality, turn to John Bond."
✏ Grayson Barber, JD, First Amendment attorney and privacy advocate, Princeton, New Jersey

"Earlier in my career I wrote what I hoped would be a roguishly different type of book on writing. Now John Bond comes along, teaches me great new lessons, and one-ups a good lot of the 'old reliables.' Without any flibbertygibbet language or hot-air-based cheerleading, Bond gives book wannabes and seasoned scriveners plenty of timely, fresh insights, true-grit tips—all wise and all's fair. His book riveted and reinspired me."
✏ Tova Navarra, author of *The Kids Guidebook: Great Advice to Help Kids Cope* and 20 other books

You Can Write and Publish a Book

Essential Information on How to Get Your Book Published

John Bond

Published by Riverwinds Publishing

Dedication

For Andrew, Kevin, Peter, and mostly Theresa.
Thanks for all you do and who you are.

ISBN: 0-9767488-0-0

Bond, John H.
You can write and publish a book : essential information on how to get your book published / John Bond.
p. cm.
Includes bibliographic information and index.
ISBN 0-9767488-0-0

1. Self-publishing-United States. 2. Publishers and publishing-Handbooks, manuals, etc. 3. Authors and publishers. 4. Authorship-Handbooks, manuals, etc. 5. Authorship-Marketing. 6. Books-Marketing. I. Title.

Z285.5. B6 2005
070.593-dc22 2005903381

The author, editor, and publisher cannot accept responsibilities for errors or exclusions or for the outcome of the application of the material presented herein. There is no expressed or implied warranty of this book or information imparted by it.

The author of this book is neither an attorney nor an accountant. Before you make any decisions that are legal or financial nature, please seek professional advice from the appropriate qualified professionals. The author, editor, and publisher are not responsible for decisions made in these and other areas and do not purport to offer advice in them.

Printed in the United States of America

Published by Riverwinds Publishing

Last digit is print number 10 9 8 7 6 5 4 3 2 1

CONTENTS

ACKNOWLEDGMENTS

To the hundreds and hundreds of people who I have spoken with over the years to try to answer their questions about how to write a book. They posed terrific questions and made me realize how much (and how little) I know. Every dinner, every lunch, every cup of coffee, every cab ride, or every walk down the street taught me about what people want from writing a book and what they want from a publisher. My thanks for their friendship and time.

To Peter Slack, who taught me more about business, publishing, and marketing than any other person in my life. He taught me about long-term relationships with good authors and doing right by everyone you run into. My thanks for all the opportunities you have provided me at SLACK Incorporated.

To people like Jan Nathans, Tom and Marilyn Ross, Judith Applebaum, John Kremer, Dan Poynter, Fern Reiss, and countless other publishing and marketing gurus. They are on the front-line everyday telling little (and big) people how to achieve their dreams of publishing and selling their ideas. My thanks for their inspirational example.

To Connie and Artie Bond, my parents. They raised four kids and worked at providing a good home to create good people. They succeeded. To my brother Art Bond and my sisters Liz Morton and Sue Morwald, who have helped make me who I am, while putting up with a nutty younger brother. My thanks for their support.

To Lauren Plummer for editing and layout. Your excellent advice and expertise improved the book from the moment you started work on it. To Linda Baker for the cover design. After so many great covers, I am always amazed how you outdo yourself.

To the reviewers of the manuscript and for their valuable feedback, thanks to: Dorothy Allen, Linda Baker, Grayson Barber, Nancy Beauchemin, Bill Blake, Paul Blake, James Bond, Greg Bussy, William Carrigan, Joe Celli, Harry Charles, Maureen Compagnoni, Len Daws, Marie Downes McDonald, Michelle Gatt, Bob Gray, Will Harley, Jane Hughes, Jennifer and Al Kilpatrick, Carrie Kotlar, Walt LeVan, Johnny May, Jim Monsu, Liz Morton, Sue Morwald, Tom Murray, Tova Navarra, Patti Perry, Eric Savitch, Robert Scott, Tom Scott, Barry Seibel, Henry Singer, Debra Toulson, Janice and Les Verhoek, Lisa Warner, Mark Warner, Jackie Woolley, and many others. You have made the words better.

To my sons, Andrew Bond, Kevin Bond, and Peter Bond. You guys are the best. You have given me more than I have given you. My thanks and admiration.

Finally, to my wife, Theresa Bond. There isn't enough paper or ink to list what you have done for me. My thanks for being who you are.

Foreword

Communication is the essence of being human and is a critical part of our daily lives. We meet so many people during our lifetime; most only briefly while others we know for years or even decades. Communicating your thoughts or message to the people you meet in a clear and concise manner allows you to express yourself properly and makes your day-to-day interactions more productive and more enjoyable.

Maybe you need to communicate your thoughts to more than one person at time. Perhaps you have dreams of communicating by writing a book. Maybe you want to tell your story or talk about your passion or hobby. Maybe you have developed an expertise that you want to share with other people. How do you move from communicating your thoughts into a polished, well written and published book?

John Bond has the answers. In *You Can Write and Publish a Book: Essential Information on How to Get Your Book Published*, he outlines the exact steps needed to take a vague idea or wish and have it become a concrete, published work. He effectively communicates what you need to know to become a published author. His 20 years of professional experience in publishing serves the readers well by condensing the world of publishing into exactly what the potential author "needs to know."

John uses a unique quiz as a tool for a potential author to quickly assess their "publish-ability" quotient. This allows you to build on your strengths and work on those points that need shoring up. When I took the quiz, it opened my eyes to the skills I already possessed as a communications professional.

I recommend you read and use this book if you:

- dream of becoming a published author,
- need the essential facts to navigate the technical aspects of finding an agent and a publisher,
- want to find out the secrets on writing and editing a manuscript,
- want to learn how you find the time to do fit this into your life, or
- want to learn how to communicate your message or ideas to thousands of people.

Take the plunge and read *You Can Write and Publish a Book* now. It will help you start down the road to becoming a published author. You won't regret it.

Thomas Murray
Senior Vice President
McCann - Erickson Advertising
New York, NY

Preface

Sharing Your Experiences; Living Your Dream

I heard an interesting thought one time: "When an older person dies, a library dies with them." I look at people I have known who have died in old age (and unfortunately some in not so old age). The experiences they have had, the things they have seen, have made me wish their thoughts could be passed on.

My Mom and Dad lived through the Depression as children and young adults in Brooklyn and Queens, New York. My Dad lived through World War II in the South Pacific. Not as a famous war hero, but as someone who experienced the war day in and day out and risked his life. They raised four kids and lived a full life. Once gone, the details of these experiences are limited to memories passed along to their friends and family.

The desire to write down these experiences or thoughts on life, whether for publication or just for your family's sake, spurred me to write this book.

I have worked in publishing for 20 years and helped hundreds and hundreds of people put their work and expertise down on paper. I have answered many questions, from how to turn an idea into a book to how to get people to buy them.

As an ex-librarian and avid reader, I am enamored by words and how they can help us communicate or learn. Books nowadays are more available, diverse, and exciting.

I truly believe most adults are able to write and publish a book. It could be about their hobby or their hometown, or even a novel. It requires time and perseverance. Most people have the tools within them right now; all they need is someone to show them the path. I hope this book can do that for you.

I think there is an audience for most books. The Internet has altered modern day American life in many ways. I love to tell the story about my Mom and eBay. She bought a book that caught her fancy at a yard sale for $1. She did not buy it as a shrewd investment. It was the story of the Flying Tigers who flew bombers during World War II. She later realized it was signed by the pilots and Chiang Kai-Shek.

She eventually listed it on eBay and sold it for $900! Pre-Internet, it would have been difficult to find someone, even a rare book dealer, to pay $100 for the book. The Internet married someone who happened upon an item with someone for whom it was the Holy Grail.

In a similar way, your work, whether fiction or your life story or about your hobby, can find its audience better than ever before. It simply requires that you determine who wants the book and how to find them. I hope this book can help you understand the concepts of finding your market and selling your book.

Write your book. Find your audience. Live your dream.

INTRODUCTION

It is Really Short. Read It.

This book is for the novice. If you have published books already or are a professional writer, it may not be for you. You might learn something from it, but the fledgling author will benefit the most.

This book is for the curious. You may have thought about writing and may have even tried your hand at it. Perhaps you have an idea or concept you would like to see published. Maybe you do not have a firm idea yet, just a vague notion.

This book is for you if you are looking for the basics on how to get started. You may need encouragement or direction.

This book is for you if you are interested in non-fiction, but many of the concepts can apply to writing fiction as well.

This book is for you if you want to write a book and become a published author.

The Self-Assessment Quiz in Chapter 2 will help you determine your "qualifications" and skills you will need to write a book. It has simple, fun questions that will help you find out where you stand in relationship to your fellow potential authors. Take the Self-Assessment Quiz with a light-hearted, positive attitude. Think about the questions and how they relate to what you will need to be an author.

After you have graded your results, move on to creating a proposal, finding a publisher, and maybe an agent. Once successful, you will move into writing your manuscript, having it become a book, and then marketing it.

I suggest you read the entire book before you start to work on any one of the steps. Get the whole picture.

Start to develop a plan and a timeline. How do you eat an elephant? One bite at a time. Also, read lots of magazines and books on publishing and marketing. Talk to other people about writing. Hang out at bookstores or libraries or wherever your target audience congregates.

Think it, believe it, and you can become a published author.

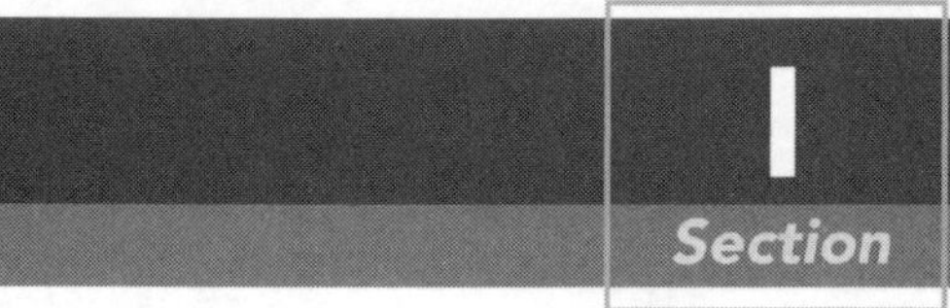

You Can Become a Published Author

1

Writing a Book is Simpler Than You Think

81% IS A BIG NUMBER

Have you ever asked yourself, "Could I write a book?" If you have, then you are in good company. It is not just famous experts, or highly creative types, or Oprah's personal trainer who write books. Publishing is open to enormous numbers of people. What usually prevents someone from moving beyond the initial idea to actually writing a book is self-doubt, ignorance of the process, or lack of commitment.

In 2002, a major publishing services company released a startling study. It found that 81% of Americans felt they had a book in them! That's over 230 million people who might write a book.

The results of the scientific survey conducted by the Jenkins Group (www.bookpublishing.com) found this surprising statistic to be true across almost all groups: men and women, most income levels, most educational levels, and many age ranges.

Imagine 81% of everyone you know being interested in writing a book. And it is possible.

Book publishing has never been easier. Whether through the larger, more well-known publishers or via smaller, regional ones, more books are being published than ever before. Self-publishing is flourishing. Becoming a publisher has a very low barrier to entry. Compared to starting your own television station or creating your own newspaper, book publishing is straightforward and very achievable. With a computer and a few dollars, the quality of your product can easily rival that of the larger firms like Random House.

What you might write about is as varied as there are different types of people in your town. Think of the different jobs and hobbies all of your friends and family have and that should start to give you some insight into the number of topics that publishing covers. Imagine if you wrote about your profession or your hobby. Thinking about writing a vacation guide to your town or area? Or what about your family's history? Or a novel that has been percolating in you for years? The list of possibilities is endless.

Many people become nay-sayers on the idea when they start to think about how much interest there would be in whatever they would write about. "Oh, no one will want to read anything I wrote." Nothing could be further from the truth. As the Information Age has exploded, the number of books has as well. This has lead to the expectation of increased specialization in all areas of life, including publishing.

Let's say you are a gardener. Of course, there is one simple book on the basics of gardening. But most gardeners would expect there to be a book for vegetable gardens and a different one for flower gardens. In the area of vegetables, they would also expect there to be a book just for tomato plants. They would maybe even expect a book would exist for specific varieties of tomato plants, let's say Big Boys. And you know, they would be right, because all of those books do exist. Now multiply all that specialization in all aspects of American life, and that's a lot of books and a lot of topics to be covered. And a lot of authors are needed.

What you need to acknowledge is your expertise. Most people will scoff at being called an expert, but most people are an expert on something. Either on the job, or with a hobby or sport, or at the very least, with their family's history. You are an expert. And experts can and do write books all the time. You simply need to acknowledge your expertise.

If you do not have one exact book topic burned into your mind, feel free to graze over the possibilities. You may want to take a few minutes to list everything that might be a topic for a book you might write. List your jobs, the current and past ones. List your hobbies. List what academic areas you have studied. List what activities you do with your kids. List where you have traveled. List what character traits you're known for, like being frugal, or organized. Examine this list and see the possibilities that start to emerge that can suit you for writing a book.

TAKING THE MYSTERY OUT OF THE PROCESS

Writing a book and getting it published, to most people, is not only a very daunting process, but also one filled with mystery. It appears to be complex and beyond the grasp of all but a very few professionals, Ivy League grads, and starving artists.

This is simply not true. You have shown an interest in the process by picking up this book. You have obviously considered the idea and are intrigued by the possibilities. Do not let the mystery stop you from proceeding—because there is no mystery. It is simply achievable steps.

Writing a book does not mean, in most instances, sitting down and writing an entire book, and then trying to find a publisher. In most instances, you will create a proposal and some sample material to show to a prospective publisher or agent. Novel or fiction writing is an exception to this method.

The steps of how to think of an idea, write a proposal, contact an agent or publisher, write a manuscript, and then proceed to publication are so straightforward that the steps can be sketched out on a single piece of paper. All the major steps can be assigned timelines, and taking it in small increments, your goal of writing a book can be achieved.

The goal of this book is to make these steps clear and understandable. Yes, there is a fair bit to learn, but it is not calculus or nuclear physics.

The process does require time and persistence. For the people who fail, it is usually due to lack of dedication or becoming discouraged too quickly. Yes, you can do it, but likewise, no one is going to call you on the phone pleading with you to write and publish a book with them. If someone has called, you are in very select company—get moving. Almost all the tools and variables to achieve this goal are within you.

Doubting Thomas?

Still not sure you can write a book? Do you not see yourself as an expert on any topic? Do you doubt anyone would be interested in what you have to say? No time or energy to do this? It is no surprise that you are skeptical. Before you read the chapters in this book that lay out the steps on how to create a manuscript and get it published, there is one assignment that may help *you* convince *you*.

The next chapter contains a Self-Assessment Quiz. It has a wide variety of questions; some are pretty easy to answer, and others are subjective. After you take the Self-Assessment Quiz, you will score it and gauge where you stand using the Results in Chapter 3.

The Self-Assessment Quiz is meant to make you think, but also for you to have some fun. I hope you view this as the promising start of a new and exciting venture.

2

Take This Self-Assessment Quiz

Why Take the Quiz?

Hopefully, this Self-Assessment Quiz will give you insights into yourself and whether you have what it takes to write *and* publish a book. It will help you examine your chances, motives, skills, and background. It will also help you assess if the odds are in your favor or against you.

This isn't a scientific quiz that has been validated to guarantee your book will be published—that can't be done. Luck and chance play too much of a role. But it will educate you to the important aspects of whether you are *more likely* to succeed. Many of the items are subjective. Be honest and light-hearted about it. This isn't the SATs. Remember, who gets published and who doesn't, who has a best-seller and who doesn't, CANNOT be predicted no matter what anyone says, including me. Even if you self-publish your book, it does not mean anyone will buy or read it.

The Self-Assessment Quiz is geared slightly toward non-fiction (for example, cookbooks, memoirs, self-help books, technical or professional material) but it can also apply to fiction. Answer every question, even if you think it does not relate to your project.

Let's Do It

Cover the Quiz Score column on the right side of the page. Mark your answer to each question in the Answer column as yes or no. Complete the whole Self-Assessment Quiz. When you are done, see the next section on scoring. Have fun!

Scoring the Quiz

Uncover the right hand column. Look over your answers and the number that has been assigned to each answer. For every answer that was a Yes, add or subtract the amount indicated. For every No, do nothing. Subtotal each area, then create a grand total at the end. The highest possible score is 264.

Some of you are going to complain about the questions that don't apply to you. Someone will say, "I am writing a book on birthday party ideas for pre-schoolers, so why does it matter if I ever spoke in front of an audience?" Take it easy. This is a fun activity meant to make you think.

Now take a break. When you are done you can move onto the Results.

3

Review Your Results

And Here Are the Results

Now that you have added up your score, compare your results to the scale below:

- If you scored 26 or below, you have some challenges. They may be in the area of commitment, skills, or expertise. Examine the subtotals by sections and compare yours to the subtotals. Focus initially on what you scored well on. Maximize these strengths. Look then at the ones you scored lower on. Concentrate on how you can improve your odds in these areas. While your chances may be lower, almost anyone can still achieve book publication. It may require self-awareness, a greater determination to work hard, and lots of perseverance.
- If you scored between 27 and 40, then you have weak areas but also some strong ones. Examine the subtotals by sections and compare yours to each one. Come up with a plan to improve your chances in the areas where you need help. Also, realize the

outcome is not set in stone, and through your personal efforts you can make this dream become a reality.

- If you scored between 41 and 52, you have a good to very good chance of being able to publish a book. You will need to concentrate on your strengths. After reading this book, lay out a timeline and game plan for your book. A journey of a thousand miles begins with a single step. Realize that you have got a challenge ahead of you, but one that is achievable for you. Become dedicated to the idea of publishing your book.
- If you scored 53 or 66, you have a very high probability of being able to formulate a book idea, find an agent or publisher, and bring the project to fruition. The chances are in your favor, and the only roadblocks are commitment, fear of getting started, or time. Take these results as a positive sign. Read this book and get started today. In a few months, you could be sailing along toward a bright horizon of being a published author.
- If you scored above 67, get writing.

Let this all sink in. DON'T stop reading here if you got great, good, average, or not so good news. Please go on to the next section and read these very important points that will help you cast your Results in the right light.

Sometimes You're Lucky, Other Times You're Not

It is a fact of life that everyone looks at where they could have been. If you scored 63 on the Self-Assessment Quiz, you probably read the score for the group above you and looked at it with envy. You *must* accentuate the positive here. Focus on the areas in which you did well, no matter how high or low your score.

No one is a sure thing in publishing! Unless you are Stephen King or Anne Rice, there are no guarantees. People with very high scores can miss the mark because of life events that get in the way, or lack of focus. People with low scores can get published through dogged determination and scrupulous planning and following the process. Do *not* stop reading and do not stop considering the idea of writing a book if you get a low score. Read the book, and try to execute the steps in Chapters 4 through 12. Then reassess your chances.

In regard to success, fortunately or unfortunately, achieving best-seller status is very elusive. Luck and being in the right place at the right time plays a huge role. If you did get a high score, temper it. Selling lots of books is really, really difficult.

Remember, if you have a complaint about a question, lighten up. This activity is meant to make you think. A low score does not mean you cannot write and publish a book, and a high score does not mean you have it made. I have given the Self-Assessment Quiz to many people. Usually the results point to a person's chances of success. But not always.

Make a Plan

Over 200,000 books are published each year. Those who *think* they can do it, can make it happen. It takes mental commitment, along with time and dedication. Take that step and try to make it happen. Even if the Self-Assessment Quiz Results say otherwise.

Read the next few chapters and while you are doing that, start to make a written plan. Write out your ideas, create a timeline, and list the tasks you have to do. Start today.

It is Easy to Get Started

4

Examine Your Motives

THE JOURNEY BEGINS

You have taken the Self-Assessment Quiz and tallied the Results. You have assessed your chances and you are going to forge ahead. Good for you. The journey will be enlightening; full of opportunities, joys, and some frustrations. The rewards may be great and the journey itself can make it all worthwhile.

Where do you start? I suggest that you begin by knowing your reasons for taking the journey. You will need to examine your motives. Sit down and make a list of why you want to write and publish your book. This list can be for your eyes only. List each reason in a few words. Make an actual list, as there will be multiple reasons on multiple levels for starting a project.

Be honest with yourself. Some of the reasons may be altruistic (to help people) while others may seem self-centered (to make money or become famous). Whatever the reasons are, write them all down.

Your list of reasons might look like this:

- I want to make money.
- I want to be famous.
- I want to publish the results of my work to gain the acceptance of my peers.
- I want to help people who do not understand the topic of my book.
- I want to write a book to help with my business and to demonstrate that I am an authority on this subject.
- I want to leave a legacy of my thoughts and experiences for my family and future generations.
- I need to express these feelings I have in order to grow as a person.
- I have a unique, imaginative story to tell that will captivate people.

This exercise will require you to look within yourself and face your motives. Perhaps you have been motoring along feeling that writing a book is simply your destiny. This exercise might make you realize that you actually would love to make big bucks out of the effort. Or that seeing your name in print to validate your ideas is essential. Honesty is the best policy here. Be true to yourself and your efforts. Get going.

Once you are finished with your list, let it sit for a day or more and then come back to it. Look at it with a fresh set of eyes to see if it is comprehensive. Ideally there will be multiple reasons for writing your book. Few people will have just one or two reasons.

So I Have This List...

Take your list and evaluate its authenticity. Does it ring true about yourself and your ideas? Now put the reasons in order from the most important to the least important. The best way to do this is to ask yourself if you achieved only one of the goals, which would be the most essential one? Then do this with each point on the remaining list until you have them all in order.

Think about the goals at the top of your list. Can they be achieved through other means? If you were looking to be recognized as an expert in a field, would being a speaker achieve the results? If there are multiple paths to the same goal, are your skills and interests best suited to achieve this goal by book publishing, or perhaps by an alternate route? You might achieve the same goal faster or easier with alternate methods.

Look at the list and ask yourself if you achieved all of the goals except the first one, would you consider the project successful? Do any of the goals conflict with any others? What are the obstacles to achieving your goals? Time? Money? Expertise? Evaluate and plan how to sidestep the obstacles.

Your Mother Taught You to Share

While not required, it may be helpful to share your idea with a close friend or family member. If you decide to do this, use someone whom you trust, and more importantly, someone from whom you can accept frank and honest observations. Ask his or her opinion of the project. Ask about your motivations. See if he or she suggests additional ones that you did not include. He or she might also suggest ones you listed that may need to be revised or altered.

Carefully consider the feedback. Close examination is a difficult thing to do, and even more difficult to accept if it contradicts your perception of yourself.

Encouragement is important. If you choose to share the list, pick a positive, upbeat person, but one who is honest. Publishing a book is an extremely achievable goal if you are willing to spend the time and effort and have perseverance.

I am amazed by the nay-saying that I read in some books about your chances to publish a book. Most of the people who say this are published authors, agents, or editors.

You need to dream and to dream big. Expect the world, but also expect to work long and hard. However, if one of your goals is to be a *New York Times* best-selling author, and you do not make it, you will find that publishing a well-received, popular work is still a tremendous accomplishment.

Visit Bermuda, Collect Rare Coins, or Publish a Book?

Perhaps you will choose to self-publish your work. If so, the barriers to publishing are only your own dedication, time, and money. Your work can spring to life based on your efforts, and you can help direct it to its ideal audience. The mythical maze of finding a publisher or agent drops away.

I am amazed by the money that someone can spend on a luxury vacation or a hobby, and not realize that for about the same cost, he or she could publish a book. The publication of your book could well exceed the enjoyment and satisfaction of either a vacation or a hobby.

Now, this cost does not count the hours spent by you to create the book and market it. These hours and days can become your part-time job, your new hobby, or your raison d'être.

The Single Thing

In the final analysis, whatever the Self-Assessment Quiz said, the final predictor of success will be your dedication. Tenacity, self determination, and resolution are the magic variables. These will be the factors that make your idea become a reality.

At one time, your parents might have said, "you can do anything that you put your mind to." At one time it was true. I wanted to be an astronaut. It still sounds fun. But I have to face reality. At my age, this is not likely to happen (at least in this lifetime). Becoming an author, however, is one thing that it is never too late to do.

Start with a dream and an idea, assess your reasons for wanting to make it a reality, roll up your sleeves, resolve to finish the task, and make it happen. It will happen.

Note: the process-oriented chapters in this book will contain a brief listing of the three key points that you should have gleaned from them. Use them to help develop a plan of attack.

If you were taking notes...

1. Honestly list your motives for wanting to write a book.
2. Share your list with a couple of very close friends, family, or co-workers to get their feedback.
3. Dedication will be the determining factor of whether you succeed.

5

Determining the Topic of Your Book

YOU EITHER KNOW IT ALREADY, OR...

To some of you, this chapter may seem silly. You probably picked up this book because you have an exact idea in mind. Perhaps you have the structure or outline of the book in your mind. Heck, you may even have a title.

Or, you may know that you would like to write on a particular subject area. Maybe it is an area that consumes your day at work or your leisure time.

Finally, some of you may just want to be an author and have not yet determined what topic suits you best. Or maybe you love to write and just are interested in a career change, possibly as a freelance writer or book author.

You will need to commit to a topic, knowing that you can always adjust your subject as you develop the book.

Think of Everything That is You

To get started on choosing a topic, make a list about you. Make a list of the jobs you have had, your hobbies, your upbringing, your personality traits, and your dreams. Include not only what you do, but also the tasks or skills at which you excel. If you are a baker, maybe your specialty is baking cookies. Maybe you are in sales, and you are very good at closing the sale. Or how about a high school teacher, and your strong point is running after-school activities. These examples can translate into the following books: cookie baking secrets from the expert, closing the sale from a master, or how to run an after-school club that's fun and educational.

Your list should not just be a mini-resumé of your life, but a descriptive and subjective look at your likes and dislikes. Maybe you are very organized, or very sloppy. Either could lead to a book. The *Sloppy Person's Guide to Organization* would be a natural.

How about family circumstances? My brother and sisters and I recently had to empty my parents' house and sell it. I wondered at the time if there were people in my situation who might be interested in hearing about how we did it.

Keep making lists. Think outside the box. Have blue-sky sessions with yourself or your friends and family. After you have your list of everything connected to you, it is time to prioritize it. Use a combination of what you are best at and what you feel most comfortable writing to prioritize it.

Do not naturally gravitate toward what you want to write about first. Start to think about what people want to read about. The old adage is "write about what you know." This is only true if people want to *read* and *pay* for what you know about.

To find out which topics have many books and which have few, try looking in your local bookstore or at on-line sites like amazon.com and barnesandnoble.com. Books on computer software are much more popular than home computer repair. Travel guides to California are more popular than ones to Iowa. Italian cookbooks win out every time over Polish cookbooks. Do all these choices seem obvious to you? Good, that means you are already thinking about what people want.

If you have an idea for a traditional Polish cookbook, do not be discouraged that Italian cooking will outsell it. Are you a member of a Polish-American society? Do you have connections to a Polish-American web site that sells books? Do you give cooking demonstrations at county fairs on Polish cooking? If so, then your book idea is a natural.

If you do research on your topic and find few books in your area, that is not necessarily bad or good news. What matters most is your take on the topic, and your ability to help find the audience. Future chapters will discuss defining your idea and your market.

Pick a topic for your book. Do not be afraid to make a choice. It is early in your publishing process. You can always start over. Now, believe it or not, is a good time to develop a tentative title.

If you were taking notes...

1. Make a list of your background and interests.
2. Include jobs you have had, the areas you excelled in, and your special interests.
3. Review how many books already exist on your top choice for a topic.

6

Coming up With a Title for Your Book

Already?

"I only just decided I should write a book. I just came up with an *idea*, and you want me to come up with a title right now? What if my book changes while I am writing it?"

Take a breath. I know this sounds like an important task, and one that you might feel is out of order. It is, however, an important step. Realize that while it should be done now, it is not set in stone.

This task applies to primarily non-fiction works. The title should come after your first full draft if you are writing a novel.

If you are writing non-fiction, creating a title this early in the process will help you focus on what your book is about. Many people are unhappy about the current state of American society insisting that everything can be defined in a few words. Many topics, people will claim, are so complex that they can't be boiled down that way. While this may be true for certain topics, it should not be the case for most non-fiction books. People will need to quickly grasp what your work is about.

When the book is first published and you are asked by a stranger or acquaintance what it is about, you may go to great lengths to describe it. Many people will not want that level of detail and will tune you out. As time goes by, you will start to voluntarily pare the description down. You will learn what parts of the description connect with people and help them to quickly understand your book.

The title is more important than almost anything having to do with your book. Accept this fact. Treat the title with respect and the importance it deserves.

Good, Great, or Fabulous

If you are going to spend too much time on any of the tasks, this is the one. The differences between a good and great title are quickly apparent. And if you are fortunate enough to think up a fabulous title, you will know it instantly when you see it on the faces of the people who hear it.

Examples of fabulous titles include:

- *Men are From Mars, Women are From Venus;*
- *Everything You Always Wanted to Know About Sex But Were Afraid to Ask;*
- *How to Win Friends and Influence People;*
- *Think and Grow Rich;*
- *When Bad Things Happen to Good People;*
- *Rush Limbaugh is a Big Fat Idiot;*
- *What to Expect When You're Expecting.*

Strive to have a fabulous title.

To get started requires some introspection. What is your book about? What is the most important part to you? To your reader? What are the secondary topics, that while important, won't be immediately evident in the title? For example, while this book covers writing a title for a book, it is not immediately obvious that it is discussed here, judging by this book's title.

Take the time necessary to think about what you really want to write. Think about what you want to focus on. You will undoubtedly come to a crossroads and will need to make some important decisions.

The task of creating a title, however, is not final. Write one as if it is the permanent one, but be aware it may, and is likely to be, revised or tweaked as the book becomes a reality.

Test Drive

Start out by making a list of key words or phrases that cover the subject of your book. Think of synonyms or common phrases associated with the topic. At first, be willing to take risks on off-beat ones. Keep your creative juices flowing.

After you have made your list of key words and possible phrases, start to play with their order. Be open to different perspectives and don't become married to the first one you like. Be willing to start from scratch.

It is helpful to make a list of common expressions, clichés, and quotations that might work with your topic or title. Be open-minded and cast a wide net. Think about words associated with the book and perhaps look them up in a quotations book. Be careful, however, of going too far and being too cute or trite.

Most books will have a title and subtitle. They will be separated by a colon. The title will be the most important part. The subtitle will come after the colon and help to clarify the topic of the book. The subtitle can be longer than the title. An important note is that the title should explain the book completely by itself because sometimes they may not appear together. Some directories, web sites, and booksellers only list the title and not the subtitle. Tell some people just the title first without the subtitle and see their reactions. See if they can determine the topic of the book.

It may help to browse through the aisles of a large bookstore. See how other people browse in a bookstore as well, and which books are picked up. I would advise staying away from the books in your topic area. Be original. You will gain more from examples of books on other topics.

Come up with a list of five or more titles that you think work. Some words or phrases may be common from title to title. Rank them in the order you like them from most to least.

Now, you will need some outside opinions. Start with a group of trusted friends or acquaintances, and run the list by them. Ask them which they like and which they don't like and why. Ask them what they think the book is about. Make notes on everything and be open to all ideas.

As you use this feedback to refine your ideas, you should narrow down your possible titles to two or three. Keep asking people, but make sure the group becomes more diverse. Ask people at parties, on the soccer field, at school, at work, or wherever you meet them. If you have a small group that is available to you, hold a mini-focus group. Keep refining until you have a title that you like that works for you.

One final step is the Google test. Think about how easily your title can be spelled. How can the words be confused or juxtaposed? If someone puts the key words in Google or other search engine incorrectly, what would the results be? Go to amazon.com or barnesandnoble.com or other on-line booksellers and put the title into the Advanced Search option. What comes up? What if words are left out or transposed? What if they are misspelled? Avoid non-essential words that are difficult to spell or not in an average person's vocabulary. You may want to ask a few people to spell the most difficult words in your title.

Remember, when you settle on one, it can still change. However, for the time being, consider it final.

Writing a Fabulous Book Title: A Brief Guide for Creating the Title of Your Dreams

Here are some pieces of advice for helping you create your ideal title. Remember, for every piece of advice or rule, there are exceptions.

- The shorter the better.
- It should be easy to remember. Tell it to a couple of people and see if they remember it a few minutes later. Check with some of them the next day to see if they remember it.
- Do not become attached to any one title, or part of a title. Be open to all ideas.

- Think of the title as a tool for marketing and sales as much as a descriptor of your content.
- Try to make the title positive. Unless it is a book on a controversial topic, people want to feel there are positive answers to problems. There are exceptions.
- Try to avoid a title that is overly cute, or one that uses a very trendy word. Titles that capitalize on trendy terms may date the book too quickly. Exceptions are if the book is focusing on that trend.
- Avoid words with accent marks like genré or non-English words like raison d'être. Most people will have a tough time spelling it.
- Avoid dates or words that date a book to a period of time. Plenty of books used the word millennium in the title a few years ago, and now it seems dated.
- When you have your final title, say it aloud many times to see how it sounds, and how easy it is to say.
- As a final task, compare your title to other books in this area to make sure you have not consciously or unconsciously created one that mirrors a rival book.

Enjoy having a title for your book, because now you will need to summarize your whole book in very few words.

If you were taking notes...

1. Creating an exciting title early on will help you focus on what your book is about.
2. Create a list of potential words and phrases and test them on friends.
3. Try to keep the title short, catchy, and positive.

7

Summarize Your Idea in a Few Words

One, One, Three

You have worked on several titles, run the best ones past your friends, decided on one, checked Google and on-line bookstores, and now you have a winner. Pat yourself on the back. You are on your way. By taking everything in incremental steps, you can achieve your goal.

I have asked you to focus on the essence of your book to help come up with your title. This effort will help now that you need to define your work in three short takes. Your next step is to come up with a one-sentence description, a one-paragraph description, and a three-paragraph description of the book. This is a deceptively challenging assignment.

What would you have Oprah read aloud if she offered to have you on her television show as her guest (calm down, this is an exercise, and this is *not* likely to occur) and she needed to complete the sentence, "And tomorrow on the program is an author who wrote a book that..." She will need to tell her viewers quickly and it will need to precisely convey your topic.

What would you have someone say if he or she was going to run an excerpt of your book on a web site and offered to start out with a one paragraph (four to five short sentences) description of the book? How would you describe your work?

Finally, a friend of yours said she will hand out a flier to her book club about your book. The book club members are the ideal readers for your topic. You can use up to three paragraphs to describe the book. What would you say to these potential buyers?

As with the title, do not get nervous. As you write your proposal, and then your book, all of these items can change. Again, these exercises are meant to help you focus on what you really want to say and what your book is about.

Start Out With a Table

The best way to come up with these three levels of descriptions is to create a rough table of contents. The number of chapters is not important at this stage, just getting the logical sequence down will help. The chapter titles can be just a few words to describe the topics. No need to worry about polished final chapter titles. You might list 20 chapters and the final book could have 15 or 30. This simply helps you get down what is, and what is not, going to be covered.

Take the table of contents and translate it into the three paragraph description. Remember, the first sentence and first paragraph are the most important. If the reader doesn't get past the first sentence, he or she will never get to the rest of the description. When writing this description, think about what question people will want answered about the book. Will your book be a simple guide, or a definitive work? Will it be full of pictures and illustrations or just text? Written for the novice or expert? Mostly bought at a bookstore, at a specialty store, through the mail, or some other way?

Think about these items as you focus on describing (and thereby, preparing to write) your book. This early focus will pay dividends and ease your task later.

To help you decide what your book is about, think about competitive books. Everyone says "there is no book like mine," but there is always at least one book (and most likely several) that people could buy *instead* of yours. Or they could buy nothing.

When you have a rough draft of the three paragraphs, move onto boiling it down to the one-paragraph description. Don't just take the first paragraph.

Then you can move on to the all important single sentence. Every word is precious and essential. Make sure one sentence is one sentence and not the biggest run-on, jam-packed sentence of all-time.

As you progress, you may need to go back and revise what you just created. Taking your time with each step will force you to re-evaluate what gets said and what gets left out. Many people (but not all, thankfully) choose to buy a book based on the flimsiest of factors. Take your time.

Think about the binding of the book. Will it be hard cover, a trade paperback (larger size), or a mass market paperback (smaller, regular size paperback)? Will it have wire-binding or plastic comb-binding like some manuals? And now there are many electronic options like an e-book or one for a PDA or hand-held device like a Palm Pilot.

Think about the format of your book. Workbooks, books that fit in your pocket, books containing CD-ROMs, and coffee table books are just a few of the options. Think about which one is best suited to your material.

A recent development in the book world is the rise of the used book market. Amazon.com and others have started to make a major commitment to resell books on the Internet. This is significant. When a book is resold, you don't receive royalties for these sales. If your book can be consumed or altered (for example, pages of a workbook ripped out, filled out worksheets), you might reduce the chances of your book being recirculated.

How Do You Buy a Book?

A key question for you to think about is how people buy books. If you are browsing in a bookstore in the gardening or cookbook sections and you are not searching for a specific book, how would you decide which one to buy? It is probably an intricate combination of cover design, title, price, size/appearance, familiarity with the topic and author, endorsements on the covers, and your mood.

As an exercise, go into a large bookstore and browse for a cookbook on Italian cuisine or a self-help book on depression. See where you are drawn and what attracts you. You may also ask a friend to do this exercise for you, and have him or her speak aloud what comes to mind on choosing a book. This exercise will help when you are creating your title, creating the cover, and describing your book, and most importantly how and what to write about.

I can't emphasize enough how important it is to spend time in bookstores and libraries and get to know the people that work there. Many independent (and chain) bookstore managers and employees know their customers and books very well. If they walk up to the United States history section, they can probably point to the ones that sell (and therefore the ones that don't). They may not always know what people love about the book, but they certainly know which ones are most popular.

Also, when you are in the bookstore, note the section where your book would be. Compare it to the other sections of the bookstore in size. Are the books shelved by the author's last name or by subcategory (as in history)? Ask the bookseller what is selling well in the store. What is selling well in your section? What is the biggest surprise seller? What is being displayed at the counter for impulse purchase? What is in the discount bin? Do these steps every time you go to a bookstore.

Remember this may not be applicable if a bookstore won't be the primary place your book is purchased. Even if this is the case, this exercise can still help you better understand your customers and how they choose one title over another.

Up to now, you have summarized your topic in a few sentences. You have an emerging image of your book. Looking forward, you will need to start to think about where to take your book idea and how to present it.

If you were taking notes...

1. Create a draft table of contents for the book.
2. Write a succinct three-paragraph, one-paragraph, and one-sentence summary of your book.
3. When choosing the words and phrases for these summaries, consider what you look for when you buy a book.

III

Section

Determine Who Will Publish Your Book

8

Choosing a Publisher

NEW YORK, NEW YORK OR SMALLTOWN USA?

At this stage, I recommend thinking about the type of publisher you would like to work with. This involves thinking about the advantages and disadvantages of large publishers versus small ones. You will also need to decide whether or not you want to seek out an agent. Finally, you will also need to consider self-publishing. As with the previous chapters, what you decide here is not set in stone.

The large publishing houses (Random House, Simon & Schuster, Harper Collins, Penguin/Putnam, Time Warner Books, and the like) are centered around New York, or have a New York mentality. They have published many of the books you have read over the years. What they offer most is a large distribution system. They have a long reach into bookstores and other retail outlets throughout the United States. When they talk, buyers listen.

Another advantage is the prestige that they offer. Most people would love to say, "Oh, Random House is publishing my new book."

To be honest, this is usually only important to the author as it gives you bragging rights.

The downside of the large publishers is their very size. Many times your editor or the marketing person will come and go and you may not have an ongoing personal contact with someone. Enthusiasm for your project may be high at contract signing, but the person may move on, and your project may drop in the priority list. Finally, if you do not bust out of the gate onto the best-seller list, your project may be fighting for attention on a huge list of other titles from the publisher. Remember, all those buyers will only listen if the publisher actually talks about your book. Also, the larger publishers (and even some smaller ones) will take 12 to 18 months to actually produce the book from your final manuscript.

The perception is that large publishers do not look at unsolicited manuscripts. This is mostly true. This is where agents play an important role. Agents earn their money (albeit from your share) by helping the publisher with some time-consuming and challenging tasks, such as looking through the slush pile for gems, helping authors through the publication process and keeping them on track, and running interference on problems. As a balance for this money, the agent should earn his or her fee by obtaining a good match with an appropriate publisher, perhaps a larger audience for your book, and/or greater concessions for you in your contract.

Smaller publishers may not have the name recognition of Random House, but you are much more likely to get personal attention and commitment. They have to be more committed, or they will not survive. You will probably have a personal contact and develop a relationship with that person. You will have fewer titles for your book to compete against.

One downside is that their distribution network may not be as wide. They may not be able to make sales calls on every bookstore. Their ability to put copies of the book everywhere may be reduced. They will be operating on a limited budget and trying to make each dollar spent work harder.

An important point to remember is that almost no one knows the name of the publisher for even best-selling authors. Can you name the publisher for Stephen King, Anne Rice, Tom Clancy, or the *Chicken Soup* series? If you can, you are in an exclusive group. Choose options based on what works best for your work, not a publisher's perceived name recognition.

Secret Agent

One of the most complex, confusing topics is whether you need an agent. Most people feel it is a catch-22. "They won't talk to me if I have no track record, and how can I get a track record if they won't talk to me?"

Agents are looking for new authors. If they just sat around and published the tenth book by an established author with the same publisher, it would be a pretty cushy job. They need to expand and grow their stable of authors. If you are unpublished you will also need to present yourself and your idea very well and make it stand out from the crowd.

If you are working on a technical work or in a specialized field, you may not need an agent. If you are publishing for the general or trade market, you probably will need one. See Chapter 12 for more information on agents.

How About My Garage?

A real option today is self-publishing. Technology and the Internet have created an environment where many hard-working, industrious people can create a product of equal or competitive quality to those of commercial publishers. For the price of a great vacation you too can have a garage full of books that you can start to promote and market.

Self-publishing allows you to retain control (and all the sales dollars) and determine your own fate. It is, however, hard work. You need to work longer, harder, and with some skills other than the ones it takes to write the book. Beware, there is a huge learning curve.

Self-publishing requires more of a flair for marketing and promotion. If you are *not* detail-oriented and *don't* like selling, *don't* self-publish.

Control is what attracts many people to this option. They can decide on their own cover. They can choose the paper the book will be printed on. They can determine who will get to hear about their book, and who will not. However, even with self-publishing, some issues are still out of your control. You cannot control whether a store chooses to carry your book.

Keeping all of the money from a sale makes greater sense to many people, instead of being paid a royalty of 10% or so. However, with all those dollars come a whole lot of other costs. Where will the boxes of books be stored? What kind of packaging will an order ship in? Who will ship it? Will you have an 800 number or web site from which a book can be ordered? All of these points (and many, many more) do not come free. Plus there is all of your time to manage or perform all these tasks. Or you could pay someone to do it, reducing your profit and lessening your control. You get the point.

Self-publishing, for it to be effective, has to be a labor of love. If all you want to do is concentrate on writing in your subject area, this may not be the option for you.

On the positive side, you will probably be able to create your product much quicker than the 12 to 18 months publishers can take. Also, self-publishing may lead to working with a publisher. If you are successful enough, it is not uncommon to have a publisher approach you about buying the book's rights or wanting to publish the new edition. It may also lead to them asking you to write another book. If this happens, your track record will put you on much firmer footing to discuss equitable financial arrangements.

One of the emerging options is the publishing services option and/or print-on-demand (or POD). Companies such as iUniverse, Xlibris, 1stBooks, and Trafford have created an option which combines publishing and self-publishing. They offer services which include editing, page make-up, and printing. The printing that they offer is called print-on-demand. It involves very high quality photocopying with a traditionally printed cover. They can produce as many or as few as are needed. The author pays for the books and services. They also offer limited book distribution. The product looks great and allows you to create a book quickly and bypass the publisher search.

This option has been embraced by an exploding amount of people who want to create a good product in a reasonable time period at a price. It allows them to have books to sell, offer at presentations, give to their families, or whatever they see as the end result to their project. The "publishing" they do is on a non-exclusive basis. Be careful because if having books in traditional bookstores is important to you (and I am not saying it should be), print-on-demand (POD) may not be for you. POD has limited reach (at best) here.

Some of the larger companies that provide this service are listed at the end of the book. Their web sites give a complete description of their services.

And All the Rest

Another option is a regional or university press. These really are a subset of small publishers. A regional publisher may focus on your geographic area or may give greater consideration to someone from that area. They may have the feel of a small publisher and be more interested in you because they will be able to maximize your local speaking engagements.

Also, universities often have an affiliated organization that publishes books. Some can be quite large, while others may be small. Some can be very focused on academic subjects. Look at the universities in your local area, or perhaps you are an alumni.

These two options can also be a springboard to larger publishers if your book is successful.

Don't feel that small publishers or regional or university presses will limit the availability of your book. All of their offerings are listed and available at amazon.com and barnesandnoble.com, just like Random House's books.

Another option is a subsidiary publishing or vanity press. They essentially create a book for you and charge you. You receive some copies, they pay a royalty, and claim to make the book commercially available. Almost unanimously, this is considered a non-option. In the age of the Internet, print-on-demand, and self-publishing, this option makes almost no sense.

There are also groups called book producers or packagers. They are a unique breed that will create a book, most often a coffee table-type book or highly illustrated one, for a fee. They will then take the finished product and help shop it around to publishers or agents. They will have done much of the leg work so a publisher can have a finished project quickly; one that they don't need to spend time and worry over developing. For your first project, this option is less likely to be applicable to you.

Also, there is an excellent book available at most public libraries called *Literary Market Place*. It is a yearly publication that lists publishers (big and small), agents, book producers, distributors, and a wealth of other contact information. Find it and get to know it. It will become a bible to you.

Finally, there are a couple of excellent listserves that provide a discussion on publishing. They are listed in the Appendix. If you are still on the fence about which is the best way to go in regard to publishing, these lively forums may help shed light on each of their pluses and minuses.

No one option is right for everyone. It depends on your idea, your individual circumstances, your motives, your desires and personality. No one can suggest which one is best for someone without examining their exact circumstances.

You've Decided

Now you are all set. You have made up your mind on small or large, or maybe self-publishing. You will need to create an exciting proposal. You have been making great headway and are well on your way.

If you were taking notes...

1. Consider your options for publishing. Self-publishing is right for some people who have varied talents.
2. Large and small publishing houses each offer advantages and disadvantages.
3. Specialty publishing firms offer different options for specific subject areas, such as regional or academic markets.

9

Writing an Enticing Proposal

Laying the Cornerstone

An enticing proposal is the foundation of all the other work you will do. It will help you to continue to focus on what your book is about. It will help you secure a publisher or an agent. A well-written proposal will be the blueprint for writing the book. It will be your promotional and marketing plan. If you self-publish, it is your business plan to clients, potential investors, a distributor, or a bank.

Even if you plan on self-publishing, I encourage you to create your proposal at this stage. It will help you to stay focused and provide you with guidance.

This step may take the most time of any that you have done so far, but it will prove to be time well spent. Don't rush the process or settle for a less than perfect proposal. Also, remember the discussion about using friends or relatives to review your titles. This task is equally valuable at this stage. When you are finished, have multiple people give you feedback on the proposal, in particular the overview, before you submit it to anyone.

Think of the proposal as a means of selling your idea with you as the author and not as a way of describing your project to a potential publisher.

One Step at a Time

A well-done proposal includes all of the following parts (in this order):

- *Title Page:* Includes the title of your book, as well as your contact information (name, address, phone, cell phone, fax, and email address). (half page)
- A *Proposal Table of Contents:* Lists the items in the proposal with their page number. Make sure you add page numbers to each page of the proposal. (half page)
- *Overview:* This is your opportunity (perhaps the only one) to sell your project. It includes a concise and enticing description of the book. The genesis of this section might be the three paragraph description of the book that you have already created, the difference being the style in which it is written. You will need a hook or some way to instantly grab the reader's attention. Draw them in. Present your "unique selling proposition" that tells readers why your book is perfect for them or what separates it from other books on the same topic. Think about what need is fulfilled by your book. The language and power of this section is most important. You will end it with a brief physical description of the book you want to write. An example is: "My manuscript will be 400 pages, with 15 photographs. I envision the final book being 6" X 9", soft cover, 250 pages." (three to six pages)
- *About the Author:* This gives you the opportunity to say why you are *the* person to write the book. Extol your background. Talk about your accomplishments. Don't be shy. Include as much information as necessary to establish you as the expert you are. (one page)

- *Schedule:* Talk about when you can deliver the completed manuscript. Be pessimistic. Under promise and over deliver. (one paragraph)
- *Resources Needed:* May be optional. If you need certain assistance or funding, this allows you the opportunity to make that known. The less you request, the better off you are. However, if you cannot get the book done without these resources, the publisher will need to know this up front. (one paragraph)
- *Competition:* An extremely important component, this section details the books someone might buy instead of yours. Give a bulleted list starting with a bibliographic entry for each book, and then a brief reason why yours is better or different. The Internet has been a godsend to this category. With amazon.com and barnesandnoble.com, and countless other sites, finding out who the competition is has never been easier. You can even see customer reviews at many sites that you can quote to bolster your claims. Remember, everyone thinks his or her idea is unique. Here is your chance to prove it. Also, if your book truly is the only thing on a subject, you'll need to cast this in a positive light as a tremendous opportunity to tap an emerging market. Finally, as you look at competitive books, note which ones are in multiple editions (a sure sign of success). Some best-selling books prominently proclaim right on the front cover how they are doing. "Over 1,000,000 copies in print" is a great quote to use. Another neat bit of information is on the copyright page. There are some clues on this page as to how many times a book has been reprinted. Sometimes it says which printing it is, sometimes it has a series of numbers and the last one indicates how many times it has been reprinted, with the lowest number being the current printing number. This information will help you show there is a market for your ideas. It shows people buy these books in big numbers. Use this information to your advantage. Finally, if your chosen area has a book club, it can be a treasure trove of information for competition as well as why to publish your book. (one to four pages, depending on the amount of competition)

- *The Market:* You will need to explain who is the market for your book. The more facts and statistics you can use, the better. Remember, not everyone who gardens buys books. Not everyone who gardens buys books on flower gardens. People with vegetable gardens will probably not be interested in the topic. In most cases, concentrate your facts on the United States. Professional associations, trade groups, the United States Bureau of the Census, or the Bureau of Labor Statistics can be *very* helpful in providing market data. The publisher will create a tentative profit-and-loss statement for the book. Why not make this process easier (and your acceptance more likely) by providing the information on market size. (one page)
- *Marketing and Promotional Plan:* A publisher will want to know what activities are necessary to sell the book. This does not mean they will agree with it, but it allows the publisher to gauge what you feel will make the book a success. You will also list what activities you plan on creating or participating in. It is part of the publishing industry's expectation that the author will not create a book and wash his or her hands of it. A publisher will want to know that the author may be speaking about the book, or may have a web site that features the book, or will buy copies for resale to the author's contacts or customers. A strong Marketing Plan with significant commitments by the author can be very influential in making a potential publisher interested. (one to two pages)
- *Table of Contents:* This is your polished version, with an exact listing of the number of chapters and polished chapter titles. If the book changes when you write it from 12 to 13 chapters, the publisher will not care. The publisher *will* care if it goes from a 300 to 500 page manuscript. Be diligent in making sure you have got the natural order of the material and what will be covered. Other changes may occur; don't sweat it. Just make sure the publisher is apprised of them. (one to two pages)

- *Chapter Outline:* This gives a description of each chapter. Do not brush this off. Spend the proper time with it. This outline could be a highly influential factor in someone deciding whether or not to pursue the book. (two to five pages)
- *Sample Chapter(s):* You will need to submit approximately one-tenth of the book. Choose those chapters that are most representative of the book or that show the material in its best light. These chapters will allow the reader to see your style. Are you coming from a folksy approach, or a just-the-facts style? It will also allow the publisher to see if you are presenting material in depth, or just touching on the highlights. (about 25 pages)

Creating the Calling Card

The proposal is critical, but before someone gets to the proposal, he or she has to see the cover letter first. The cover letter is different from a query letter, which is sent by itself without a proposal. See Chapter 11 for information on query letters.

The cover letter to the proposal may play an important role. Many people will scan it and then proceed to the main course without having spent much time with it. However, some people may scrutinize the letter to save the time of having to read the proposal. Write the cover letter as if someone may never see the proposal. Write it as if these four paragraphs are your only opportunity to talk with a potential agent or publisher.

The opening sentence and paragraph may be a hybrid of your overview from the proposal. Tease or challenge the reader to such an extent that the reader will want to open up the proposal. Keep the letter short and succinct, but include enough facts about the book in case the reader wants to know what it is you are pitching.

Some Pointers

Quality is one of the hallmarks of success. Authors talk about why their book is better than the competition. Treat the proposal the same way. Make sure you put maximum effort into creating the proposal. Write, revise, refine. Test it out on many people. Ask them what they would change. Or where their interest wanes.

When you are writing about your book, remember to write about what your readers want not what you want to write.

Even if your book is on a technical subject, the proposal should be able to be read and understood by most people. Use a minimal amount of jargon in the proposal, unless it is absolutely necessary to convey what you will cover.

This is also a good time to revisit your title. Now that you have further defined the book, you can examine your title to make sure it is a winner and reflects your current direction. Make any necessary refinements.

There are some excellent books on writing a proposal. Some are listed in the Bibliography. I encourage you to read more about this crucial step.

Remember, publishing is a business interested in making money. Publishers are not altruists. You will need to appeal to their business side about the sales your project will generate.

When deciding what category your book fits into, make sure it is one of the major areas inside the large, chain bookstores. There is a category called reference. There isn't one called family history. You need to fit into the existing system, like it or not.

Finally, be truthful and do not exaggerate. Making your market sound much larger or wildly exaggerating the book's potential may just cause other statements you make to be dismissed.

Now What Do I Do With It?

You have created a dynamic proposal—what next? There are some small details that are very important.

- Have several people proofread it simply for grammar and spelling. Nothing will blow your credibility like misspelled wourds.
- Invest in some nice quality paper and envelopes, suitable to your subject matter and your style.
- Common wisdom says that whenever you send it to someone, include a self-addressed stamped envelope. Some people have suggested to not include one as it looks like you expect a rejection. This is your call. The actual print out of the proposal is cheap, however, I doubt anyone is deciding to publish a book based on this psychological factor.
- Before it goes anywhere, double check that it is picture perfect. Like resumés for job hunting, the person receiving your submission is looking to eliminate the amateurs who make obvious mistakes like forgetting a component, or producing it on a malfunctioning printer.

I have had people ask me if they should copyright their proposal. Others have asked what prevents publishers or agents from taking their idea and giving it to their favorite writers. For non-fiction work, this issue is just flattery of the person asking the question since there are few unique ideas in publishing.

Very few people have such groundbreaking work that has not been done by someone else in some other way, or some other area. They may think it so, but it is most likely not true. The overwhelming majority of publishers' and agents' greatest asset is their good name and reputation and stealing ideas would damage their asset. Plus, if the publisher is going to pay a royalty on the work, they are not saving any money giving your idea to someone else. If anything, it may cost them in legal fees. Worry more about making your proposal and book as dynamic as possible, instead of someone stealing your secret formula.

Despite the previous point, your proposal should be so complete that a creative person who is an expert in the field should be able to take your proposal and write a similar book. Granted it would be a different book and would not have your mark on it, but it would be close. Hold nothing back from the proposal. Let it all hang out.

Finally, remember that as you progress through the process, the proposal can be revised, added to, or tweaked. You are in for a valuable education.

You now have a dynamic proposal. Sit back for a moment and look at the progress you have made. Finding a publisher is in sight. But before you do this, it will be very beneficial if you find testimonials or endorsements from well known people in your field.

If you were taking notes...

1. A well-crafted proposal is key to finding a publisher and agent.
2. A cover letter is even more essential to getting your point across quickly.
3. Concentrate on perfection and quality to make sure every aspect of your proposal and letter are top notch.

10

Getting Great Endorsements for Your Book

Imagine

Just think if you got Oprah to say the following about your self-help book: "It changed my life." Or how about if the president of General Motors said, "The ideas in this book will revolutionize global business." Or if Emeril Lagasse exclaimed, "This book taught me more about cooking than anything else in life." Hey, it doesn't hurt to dream.

For many books, testimonials or endorsements can be the difference between success and mediocrity, or getting published versus having your manuscript sit in a drawer. Imagine the instant credibility you would have with a potential publisher or agent if you could include in your cover letter or proposal a guarantee that you could get a national radio talk show host or a Pulitzer Prize winner to write a glowing foreword to the book.

Instead of scoffing in disbelief, the only thing stopping you is yourself, some research, and time. People are always surprised to find out two facts. First, almost everyone knows someone who knows or has met someone very, very famous. This is where the concept of "six degrees of separation" originated. Second, they are amazed at just how common it is for mid-level famous people to agree to write a few sentences about your work, many times for free. These people probably remember the past when they were trying to climb the ladder as well.

Other than the time spent on your proposal, this step is one of the most essential tasks not to rush. More time spent here will increase the chances of you getting published as well as selling more books later.

How High to Shoot and Where to Shoot

Perhaps you realize that you know the leaders in your field. Many people do not know just how well connected they are. If you do not, it is time to think about who you know and who they know.

"Six degrees of separation" has become a part of our cultural lore. It started with a study about 40 years ago. People in the Midwest were asked to have something delivered to a person in Boston unknown to them. When asked to do this, they found someone, who knew someone, who knew them.

Most people do not know the president, one of the Rolling Stones, or a professional football player. However, most people have well over 100 acquaintances, taking into account family, friends, work, neighbors, and so on. Each of those people has 100 acquaintances as well and so on. You can see how quickly the circle spreads.

Start to make a list of the people you know. Some people will be very well connected while others not. Do not overlook the latter, as they only need to know one or two key people to get out of the bounds of their small circle of friends and potentially reach someone important. Think about what someone does, where they have lived, and what stories they have told over the years.

I started my list feeling like I knew no one. I realized that my sister-in-law knows someone who knows George W. Bush. Then I realized that my best friend's brother knows someone who knows the members of the band Fleetwood Mac. If you laugh and say that you are not that lucky, then you just have not spent time doing this exercise.

Keep making your list. Concentrate on the people who work in higher profile jobs or work outside your community. You may just want to list people to talk to so you can find out who they know or have met. They may surprise you.

The biggest challenge you will face is not wanting to ask friends or neighbors a favor. Maybe it has to do with not imposing on them or maybe you don't want to discuss your dream of publishing a book with them. However, you will need to get past it. Overcoming this hesitancy will be key to your success.

As your list expands, you need to continue to concentrate on your subject area. If you are writing a book on needlepoint, you do not need Bill Clinton or Tom Hanks to write a blurb. Maybe your list is easy because you are looking for the titans of your hobby or specialty field. Even if you just need the big names of your field, still shoot as high as you can.

Think also about professional or trade associations or groups that work in your area. Having the director of NASCAR write a blurb for your book on the history of race tracks in the United States would be at the top of your list. Finally, do not leave businesses off your list. The leaders of the businesses in your field will lend instant credibility, depending on the topic.

A Blurb or a Foreword

Think about what would serve your interest best, for the person to write a blurb or the foreword. Only one person can write the foreword to the book. Many people, however, can write an endorsement or blurb (two or three sentences giving his or her opinion about the content) about the book. Reserve your grandest wish or biggest name for the foreword. Remember, you will excerpt whatever they say and put it on the back cover as well. An excerpt will also go into your proposal and cover letter.

You should also target people who are connected to your topic to comment on the book for use on the front cover, back cover, first two pages of the book where the endorsements or testimonials are typically listed, as well as in any marketing materials.

Have them comment on you as the author, the content and its quality, or their take on the work as a whole and its importance. On rare occasions, someone may ask the type of comments you want. Feel free to submit a sample of what you are looking for. If this happens, be positive, but not outlandish.

The tasks discussed in this chapter can be worked on or accomplished before the proposal stage, or when the manuscript is completed. Doing it early allows you to use these actual endorsements, or agreements to do one, to gain a publisher. If it is done at a later stage when the manuscript is completed, you will have a greater number of people agreeing to a review based on being able to see the actual book.

It Never Hurts to Ask

How to ask is as important as whom to ask. If you have a passing acquaintance with the person, a phone call will be best. If you came by them from someone you know very well directly, perhaps you could ask the person to make an introductory call, with you following up after that.

When (and if) you get the person on the phone, be quick and to the point. You recently wrote a book (or are in the process of writing one), and you would be honored if the person would preview it. If it meets with his or her approval, any comments would be greatly appreciated. Offer to send the complete book/manuscript or sample chapters. For all people who agree to write a blurb or the foreword, you will need to secure written permission to use the comments in print as well as the person's name and affiliation.

If you only know the person who is introducing you in a peripheral way, a letter or email will probably be better. Mention the mutual acquaintance in the first sentence. If you receive no response in two weeks or so, you should follow up with a phone call. Mention immediately that you are following up on your letter/email and also again note the person's name who knows them.

If the person has agreed to look at it, send the material as soon as possible. When you are sending your manuscript/book for someone to comment on or to write the foreword, always send it via express delivery with companies like Fed Ex or UPS. These packages always get more attention than the regular mail. Include a letter that reminds the person about your conversation, what it is you want, and that the person agreed to look at it.

If the person is reviewing the idea, your proposal, or a section of the book prior to completion, offer to send a complete copy when you are done. Or perhaps have the reviewer agree to review it when done. This promise will be extremely valuable to include in your proposal.

If at First You Don't Succeed...

Do not be discouraged by people not returning your calls or saying no. Perseverance is the name of the game. Ask, ask, ask. What is the worst that can happen? That they say no? So what?

Most people are apt to give up too soon. The only exception is if you came by this contact via a personal friend and if the person you are asking is a close associate of theirs. Do not put your friend in an awkward position of having the person you are asking unhappy with having his or her name passed along.

However, persistence will win the day in many cases. Another strategy to use if you ask someone and the person says no, is to ask who that person can recommend who may be able to do it. If you asked the president of Coca-Cola to comment on your new business strategy book and he or she said no, maybe he or she will suggest that the vice-president might want to do it. It wouldn't be a bad second place. When this happens, mention that the first person suggested you contact them. His or her name will surely catch their attention.

Other Tactics

A key point is the importance of getting the right contact information. Many times people don't respond because they did not receive the requests. Do your research as to what is the best way to reach someone.

Sometimes famous people have their own web sites, like www.stephenking.com. See if the site provides a way to contact the author. Or look in their books and see where they live. See if they are listed in the phone book. *Don't* contact them by phone unless you have a personal connection to them. Also, search the web for other references to them. Many times sending your query to a middle man, like their publisher, can prove fruitful, or it may mean they are screening their mail. When in doubt, send it to multiple sources.

If you have secured a publisher or agent, they can be a great source of contact with quality candidates to write blurbs. Obviously, this would not benefit you by using it in the proposal, but it would surely help sell the book by having them listed on the back cover. Talk with your publisher or agent about the best people they know and how to contact them.

When all else fails and your dream list does not come to pass, you can still fill in the endorsements page with people whose professions qualify them to comment, even if their names do not have instant recognition.

Consider the local bookstore manager, or your state senator. How about a local psychologist or minister for your self-help book? Try local chefs at fancy restaurants for your cookbook. Be creative when rounding out your list. People will be honored to be asked, and probably slightly embarrassed if he or she is not famous.

After Publication

Do not stop once your book is published. You are then a published author and have even more ground to stand on to ask people. In fact, you may want to go back to those people who said no and ask again.

You or your publisher may have chosen to list the endorsements in the front of your book. Remember that as your book is reprinted (because it is selling so well), you could always add new blurbs or replace the lesser ones with your better, late addition people. It is well worth the expense to add these higher quality blurbs into the book if it will catch the attention of a greater number of readers.

Now you have a proposal and some glowing testimonials from leaders in your field. Let's find a publisher, an agent, or both.

If you were taking notes...

1. Testimonials or endorsements from famous or influential people in the field can be critical to a book's success.
2. Create a list of people you know, and people they know, and start to get a wish list of actual contacts you have who might write a quote for the book.
3. Make a list of very famous people who you do not have a connection to, and send them your best letter. You may be surprised at the ones who will take you up on your request.

11

Finding a Publisher

WHICH SHOE FITS BEST?

You have decided which works best for you: a large New York publisher, or a smaller one that will give you more personalized attention. You also thought about whether you wanted to try to find a publisher directly, or if you wanted to be represented by an agent. Now is the time to implement these decisions. As mentioned earlier, your first decision was not set in stone, and therefore can be revisited after reading these chapters.

The next chapter talks about how to find an agent. Even if your choice was to have an agent represent you, read this chapter and Chapter 12 because there will be valuable information in both that you will need to know. If you want to self-publish, you *could* skip to Chapter 15, but I would not suggest it. You might change your mind, or you might learn some new skills or techniques that will be helpful in your publishing efforts.

As previously discussed, there are different types of publishers from big to small, general to specialized. Think about your motives, your personality type, and your material.

- Are you interested in making big money on your work? Then maybe you need to concentrate on the large New York publishers. The largest firms find about 85% or more of all the books they publish via agents.
- Will a lot of marketing be done via your own efforts such as speaking engagements? Then maybe a smaller publisher will work just as well.
- Do you have a lot of connections in your geographic area? Then a regional publisher might work best.

After you have confirmed the type of publisher you are interested in seeking, you will next need to come up with a list of publishers in that category. You will also need to determine the best way to be in contact with them.

Looking Down the List

I have mentioned an essential reference book titled *Literary Market Place* or the *LMP*. This book lists all publishers with their contact information and some other valuable facts. It is a wealth of knowledge and a great place to look when you are deciding whom to contact. However, it can be an overwhelming task to determine the best one for you. There are thousands of publishers in the book, and it is tough to tell one from another after awhile. They all sound good.

So you will need to narrow down the publishers you will want to contact. There are several methods to come up with your key prospects. One of the best ways is to look for books in the same genré or on the same topic as yours. Go to a large bookstore or library. Browse through the section of the bookstore where your book would be located. Most likely you will start to notice some of the same publishers over and over.

If you come across a book that is directly competing against your book, take note. The publisher may choose not to publish your book because it might create competition with itself. This is not always true, but this may be a factor you want to consider.

Without knowing any details about you, your idea, or your market, my rough rule of thumb is that first-time authors should lean toward small or medium publishers for their first book. You are more likely to find one and more likely not to get lost in their system. There are exceptions, but this may help to guide some of your decisions.

Make a list beginning with the best prospect, down to the ones that are still interesting but of a lesser priority. Limit the list to 20 or fewer prospects. As you find better candidates, your list will change and some may be replaced by better matches. Also remember that some publishers may have merged or changed. If you find a publisher in the library that published a book from the late 90's, you will need to check in the *LMP* to see if they are still a stand alone company. Consolidation has made publishing a smaller world at the top.

If you are looking for a regional publisher, the *LMP* has a geographic index that shows which publishers are in which state. This is a great cross-reference for you to find out who is local.

You should also look at trade publications. *Publisher's Weekly* is an essential magazine for book publishing. It contains information on who is doing what and what they are publishing. It has valuable articles on publishing, sometimes gives editors' names, and often discusses agents. In addition, magazines such as *Writer's Digest* give excellent information about what is going on in the world of publishing. I suggest you subscribe or visit a library regularly to read these magazines.

Listserves and email newsletters also have become extremely valuable tools. "Publisher's Lunch" is the best one. It is informative and great fun to read, with a ton of useful hyperlinks. Some information is available for free, while other levels require a subscription fee. It has great information on editors and agents.

Finally, writing seminars or clubs can be great ways to network to find out about publishers and agents. There is a list of them in the *LMP*. They are not in all geographic areas so they may not be best for you. If you happen to be in one of those limited areas, search on the web and see if there are any virtual ones to join.

Other Rocks to Look Under

There are other, more creative ways to find publishers. Networking with writers, agents, or large bookstore managers is a good one. Do not be afraid to ask a favor of a new acquaintance.

Some people have run ads in publications such as the *New York Times* or *Publisher's Weekly*. This method is expensive and does not guarantee results. However, it can put you in touch with some publishing people.

There are also large gatherings or conventions where publishers are located. BookExpo is an annual convention for the American Booksellers Association. Publishers come to the convention to sell their new or current titles to bookstores. It is a good place to browse publishers and get ideas, and possibly introduce yourself. The largest book-focused convention, the Frankfurt Book Fair, is held in the Fall in Frankfurt, Germany. It is truly impressive in size. Publishers attend to sell rights to each other and to create foreign-language editions for other countries. As someone who has walked the halls of the Fair before, let me tell you, it can be overwhelming to the novice. However, it is a who's who of publishing. Finally, there are meetings such as the American Library Association convention, or regional book fairs or associations. They too can yield some good contacts.

In all of these places you will find publishers, both large and small, in one place for very specific reasons. They are *not*, however, looking for authors. In fact, the people you would need to talk to many times do not attend. Beware of attending any of these conferences with high hopes of striking a deal. It just won't happen. It is, however, a good place to get ideas and network.

Work ruthlessly to match your book to the appropriate publishers. Nothing is a bigger waste of your time (and the publisher's) than to receive a proposal for an area or type of book they would never consider publishing.

Your final list will start to emerge. Now you will need to know what to do with the list.

Please Mr. Postman

Take your list and go to the *LMP* and look up each publisher's entry. Make sure you have the right address and contact information. The *LMP* lists "Key Personnel" for each publisher. Some publishers will list editors to whom material should be addressed. Even if it does not list the contact person for book proposals, it can put you in touch with some people worth talking to. You can also call or email to find out where to send your material.

Also go and find the publisher's web site. Most times, sites are geared toward publicizing or selling books, but some will have information on submissions. Read carefully what they request you do, and stick to it.

You are now set to contact the publisher. You might send your proposal, or a query letter, depending on the publisher's preference or your type of project. The query letter is a hybrid of your cover letter and the overview section of your proposal. It queries the person on his or her interest in seeing the full proposal. Limit the query letter to one page, maximum. Important notes to hit in a query letter (to a publisher or an agent) are: a brief but engaging explanation of the book; why it is right for them; who you are; why it is different from what is on the market and why the market wants it; length; and timeline.

A trend that will continue to grow is to have your proposal and sample chapters on-line. If a publisher or agent shows interest because of a query, you can email them the site name or the actual documents. Make the documents password protected (and obviously provide the password). Also, offer to send them as hard copies if they prefer. See Chapter 20 for more information about other reasons to create your own web site.

Always, always address the letter to a specific person. Never address the letter to "Dear Sir or Madam" or "To whom it may concern." If you don't have an exact name from your research, call the company and ask for the editorial department. Ask to whom submissions should be addressed.

You will want to respect any request a publisher may have on simultaneous submissions. Simultaneous submission means many agents or publishers will be looking at the material at the same time. Many times, publishers or agents will request that they be the sole group looking at the material. If you do not know its policy, assume it prefers not to have them. This will require you to keep track of when you submit to a publisher, and to follow up in a timely manner and to ask for feedback. If they are non-responsive after an acceptable time period (perhaps one to two months), you can then proceed to your next candidate. If you do choose to send simultaneous submissions, make sure to note this in your cover letter.

Not all books at all publishers are bought through agents. The smaller the publisher or the more specialized the topic, the less likely this is to be the case.

When you contact publishers, you may be dealing with editors or acquisitions editors. Acquisitions editors are charged with finding and signing new projects. After you have a contract, the editor may continue to be your key contact for a period of time, but you will get to know other people as well. When an editor or acquisitions editor begins to develop an interest in your project, he or she will need approval from other people at the publisher. This may be an editorial committee, probably composed of people in management, finance, marketing, and production.

Hearing No

Rejection has become part of the whole mystique of being an author. People react in different ways, but the most common response one hears is dejection or disappointment. Sure it would be great if your first, best choice agreed to publish your book on the first try, but that isn't realistic. Rejection does *not* mean your work is bad or you are unqualified.

Even if it is a form letter, do not read too much into a rejection letter, or even several of them. There can be innumerable reasons for being rejected, many having nothing to do with you or your work. Often you will not know the true reason for the rejection. The publisher may have recently agreed to publish a book on the same topic. The publisher may have exceeded the number of titles it planned to publish in a year. You may have caught them on an off day when nothing looked appropriate for their line of books. Or you may have done a poor job of matching the publisher with the topic. Do not go to a hardware store for aluminum foil. Sure, they may have it, but you would be better off going to a grocery store. Match your efforts to the current direction of the publisher.

Move on from the rejection and keep trying. If you are lucky enough to get personal feedback about your proposal or idea, carefully consider whether to adjust your work based on such feedback. Try to be objective, while staying true to your vision of your project.

Stay persistent. You will prevail and someone will agree to publish your work.

I'm Looking for One With...

At this point in the process, you probably just want a publisher or an agent. But if given the choice, what you want is one with certain qualities or characteristics:

- Top of the list is enthusiasm for your project. Your excitement for the book should carry over to them.
- A publisher or agent should have worked with other books in your field, which demonstrates knowledge of the area, and a commitment to it.
- You want a publisher or agent that answers you in a timely manner.
- Finally, you want a publisher or agent that feels *you* are the person to write this book.

Granted, a publisher or agent that does not have all of these qualities will do. If they do not, your happiness at the prospect of being published now may be tempered by some harsh realities later.

If you were taking notes...

1. Develop a list of potential publishers well suited to your topic and interests.
2. Use creative ways to develop a list of publishers and personnel that you want to contact.
3. Rejection does not mean your project is bad. Wait for a publisher that is excited and dedicated to your project.

12

Finding an Agent

Why Do I Want an Agent?

This step will be a big question mark for many people. It may appear unnecessarily time-consuming or complex. Given the choice between going through the publication process with or without an agent, in almost all instances I would suggest (if possible and practical) using one. Obviously, if you are self-publishing, this is a non-issue. Also, for some specialized areas such as scientific/technical/medical or professional areas, agents may not be part of the normal process.

What makes many people wary of this step is the previously mentioned catch-22. How do I find an agent if he or she only represents published authors, and how can I get published if I do not have an agent? Don't despair, as most agents need first-time authors, just not as much as first-time authors need agents.

Having an agent will make your quest for a publisher easier, and publication more successful. The vast majority of agents are interested in people who present themselves well, understand and are serious about their ideas, and have a polished proposal.

What They Will Do for You

First and foremost, an agent should get your proposal looked at by the right people in the right publishing houses. For this service alone, the agent is worth the fee. Instead of spending a lot of time floundering around and learning through rejection, an agent will be able to assess your idea and if he or she is interested, marry it to the right publisher. The agent knows who is buying and in what area. The agent should also be objective, which may not be to an author's liking.

Agents ask and answer the right questions. The agent has been through the process many times, and knows why things are the way they are. The agent can educate you about the aspects of publishing that you are not familiar with. On the opposite end, the agent will be the intermediary with the publisher with your requests, questions, or problems. The agent can run interference, either way, with difficult issues.

After the agent gets your manuscript placed with a publisher and gets you a contract, his or her role will change. He or she will move from selling you and your idea, to helping facilitate manuscript submission and, ultimately, to publication.

At the top of the list of what agents get credit for is the financial deal. The agent may help you get a bigger advance or higher royalty. How far the financial issue can be pushed can, in and of itself, earn you back what an agent is paid.

If you are an unpublished author and can get an agent, the services he or she will provide are probably invaluable to you although you may not yet realize it.

Where to Look

Many of the suggestions or tactics in the previous chapter on finding a publisher will apply to agents as well. The *LMP* lists the largest, most well-known agencies that do not need to advertise their services or existence.

The web has been very helpful with finding an agent. There are some excellent sites by independent people that have a comprehensive listing of agents. Some have subjective commentary and observations. I would suggest you check them out. They are listed in the Appendix.

Another common way to find agents is to look in the acknowledgments in a book. Look in books that are in the field in which you intend to publish. Many times authors will thank their agent by name and sometimes by agency. If an author thanks an agent just by name, put the name into a search engine and see what comes up.

You can also email an author and ask him or her to refer you to his or her agent or agency. If this happens, make sure you note this in the first sentence of your letter or email to the agent.

Also, networking can be invaluable. Going to writers' conferences or seminars are ways to meet people who have agents. Briefly tell them your idea and background. Ask authors if they can suggest someone or if they know someone else to ask.

Publishers Weekly discusses specific agents in some of its articles and columns. Be prepared, though, as the agents mentioned are usually the highest profile ones. Magazines such as *Writer's Digest* can also provide valuable information about what is happening in the world of writing and publishing.

Some large publishers have part of their web site that lists subsidiary rights contacts for their larger, more important books. Subsidiary rights are using the material in other forms, such as an excerpt in a magazine, a foreign-language edition, or an audio version of the book. These web sites may list agents and their contact information

As previously discussed, the email newsletter and web site "Publishers Lunch" has a wealth of information about agents and publishers and the topics or books they are currently involved with.

Take note of who the agent is and what he or she has done. The agent's location (Manhattan or Idaho) in the age of cell phones and email has become less relevant, whereas who he or she represents (specifically in your area of expertise) and how many books recently successfully placed will tell you whether he or she is worth their salt. Unfortunately, anyone can call themselves an agent, but it doesn't mean he or she will be able to find a publisher for your book. Beware, an inferior agent is worse than no agent. An inferior agent is one who is not respected by publishers or one who can't get books placed with appropriate publishers. Potentially, you can ask for a list of references to ensure that your agent cuts the mustard. Whenever possible, try to find an agent who is a member of the Association of Author's Representatives.

At this point, using the web to research your list is helpful. See if the agent has a web site, and if so, what it says. Do not use an agent's individual site as a way to find agents. The ones that are big and successful do not need the publicity. The ones that are struggling and just starting may have big sites to pull you in. Beware.

What to Send Them

Once you have developed a list of potential agents, you will need to decide whether to send a query letter or a letter and the full proposal. See the previous chapter for information on the parts of the query letter. *LMP* recommends a query letter with an outline and a sample chapter. You may be able to check what an agent prefers by looking in *LMP* or on his or her web site. For others, it may not be readily apparent what is preferred. In these instances, start with the proposal. As with the publishers, observe any requests they may have not to receive simultaneous submissions. If you do send query letters simultaneously, note it in the letter.

When looking at your cover letter, or the query letter that you created, make sure it is adjusted to the agent's point of view, as opposed to the publisher's. The agent wants to know that you are committed to the project, have the ability to promote the book, and will follow through on your commitments. Potentially include a self-addressed stamped envelope for a reply or for the return of materials.

After two weeks, feel free to contact the person to whom you sent the package to confirm its receipt and check on its status. As with a publisher, after a reasonable period of time without a response, it is acceptable to move on to another potential agent.

With agents and publishers, keep track of to whom you sent your materials and on what date. You do not want to duplicate your efforts.

What You Owe an Agent and What The Agent Owes You

Most agents will get 15% of everything you are paid. This includes the advance, your royalty payment, rights payments for other uses, and so on. There are exceptions to these percentages, but as a rough guideline, 15% is a good ballpark figure. For those of you who are skeptical about how hard an agent works for you, remember that 15% of nothing is nothing. Most agents (unless they are charging you fees to read your manuscript) get no money if they never place your book.

Aside from the money, you owe the agent several things. You owe the agent your honest and open consideration of his or her suggestions and ideas. He or she is a neutral party and many times knows best. If an agent makes a suggestion, you owe it to him or her to listen very carefully and consider the idea. You also need to be honest, whether it is regarding a delivery date or your ability to meet the request of the publisher.

The agent owes you several things. As mentioned in the previous chapter, agents should be enthusiastic about your project. The agent needs to have a good knowledge and a track record in the area you are interested in publishing in. Finally, the agent needs to return your calls or emails in a timely manner.

You will sign a contract with your agent. It will be shorter than the one you will sign with your publisher. More on the publishing contract later. Your contract with your agent gives your permission for the publisher to deal with the agent on financial and other matters. It will state that all payments and reports will go to the agent. It will formalize the relationship you have with the agent.

An important caution. Some in the industry use fees to offset costs or to actually make money. Some agents may charge reading fees to look at your proposal or manuscript. There may be more fees in addition to these, with no guarantee that you will receive a contract if their edits are made. It is generally agreed that agents who stress these fees or have very high fees are really only offering editorial services and are not agents. Most great agents want to make money from the percentage of the advance or royalty, as opposed to just charging reading fees.

In the *LMP* the listing of agents states that reading fees might be charged. It even cautions that you should obtain full details of all fees before sending in your manuscript for further review.

Finally, there are many publishers who will not even accept or review unagented manuscripts or proposals.

In conclusion, if you have the opportunity to proceed down the road to getting a publisher with or without an agent, get one. An agent's efforts, while costing you a percentage of your royalty, will almost always make the process go smoother and better. Agents know the industry and will provide valuable assistance to you as you navigate a unique landscape.

If you were taking notes...

1. If it is possible to obtain an agent, by all means do so. It will make obtaining a publisher easier.
2. Use various methods to develop a list of potential agents to whom to send a query letter or proposal.
3. The percentage of sales an agent is owed is well-deserved payment for the objective feedback and efforts to get your book to publication.

13

Securing a Contract

CONGRATULATIONS!

You have a publisher interested in your book. Or perhaps you have signed on with an agent and the agent got a publisher enthusiastic about your idea. You have cleared a big hurdle. There is one important detail to wrap up before you pop the champagne cork: the contract.

It is not official until you have received the contract, reviewed and understood it, signed it, and the publisher has countersigned it and returned a fully executed copy to you. Prior to that, a publisher could have said yes, but gotten cold feet and reneged on the promise.

So when the contract arrives, turn the phone off, get a cup of coffee, sit down, and get ready for an education.

FIRST THINGS FIRST

If you do not regularly review legal documents, looking at a book contract for the first time can be an imposing task. The contract will be anywhere from four to ten pages in length. Many of the items discussed cover the same concepts from publisher to publisher but with different wording.

The contract is a necessary and important step. It spells out the conditions under which your book will be published. If all goes well, you will put it in a safe place and will never need to refer to it again. If things do not go as planned between you and the publisher, it should give you some understanding of your options. The contract is all about hypothetical situations, or "what ifs."

Many people will fall back on the statement that they do not understand legalese. In my opinion, most people who are able to write a book are more than intelligent enough to read and understand the concepts included in a standard publishing contract. If you do not understand what is being said in the contract: ask, ask, ask.

Read through the contract one time. Take your time and think about what concept each clause is addressing. Each clause is probably included because of some previous misunderstanding between an author and a publisher. Your goal should be to understand every clause and its intent. Do not sign the contract until you can explain it to someone else.

What to Worry About

To be honest, the standard book contract favors the publisher. Heck, they wrote it. If you are a first-time author, it will probably be even more favorable to the publisher. It favors them legally as well as financially. If this does not sit well with you, perhaps you need to consider self-publishing.

Most of the contract you receive is boiler plate, or made up of standard wording. The publisher will add your name and address, book title, manuscript due date, and other variables to your version. There is not that much that changes in most contracts, and not much of *substance* you can negotiate if you are a first-time author. Publishers on average do not significantly revise contracts because the industry sees this as a perfunctory task in the publishing process.

The publisher's success comes from all of the books it publishes, not one specific project. If you doubt whether you are getting the best deal, ask the publisher if what it is offering is what most authors receive. If not, have the publisher explain to you why it is less or different for you. Most publishers will be honest, and explain any differences to you.

To Employ a Lawyer or Not to Employ a Lawyer

Many first-time authors, with or without agents, worry about being made a fool of by blindly signing the contract. Many will consider consulting a lawyer.

As I said, most contracts are composed of standard wording with little leeway for changing the big or key points. Hiring a lawyer can be an expensive way to have it explained it to you. You should try to review it first yourself. If you have questions, start with the publisher. If you do want to consider hiring a lawyer, do so for peace of mind, not with the expectation that you will get a tremendously better deal.

If you do decide to get a lawyer, make sure he or she is one who specializes in publishing or intellectual property. The lawyer who drafted your will or who lives next door will probably not be qualified. If you hire a local lawyer not familiar with publishing, you will be paying for him or her to get educated in the area of intellectual property, and will probably not get much in the way of significant results.

Lawyers serve a valuable purpose in the publishing system. First-time authors, however, have little to no leverage. Know what the expenses will be before you sign on with a lawyer.

The Bibliography in this book lists three books about contracts and publishing law. They are well worth the investment.

Show You the Money

Royalties can be calculated in many ways. Royalties can be calculated on the list price (which is the price listed on the cover) or on the net sales (that being after the publisher gives a bookstore a discount). Being paid on the list price is obviously much more enviable, but being paid on the net sales (especially for first-time authors) is much more common.

Average royalties for hard cover books might start at 10%, and trade or mass market paperbacks might start at 7% or 8%. This varies only slightly from publisher to publisher. You could receive escalated royalties, meaning the percentage goes up as the number of copies sold does. For instance, if you sell between 1 to 5,000 copies, you would receive 10%, from 5,001 to 10,000 you would receive 12.5%, and finally 15% for everything above 10,000 copies. Once the publisher has recovered its initial costs, you should share in the wealth.

An advance is an up-front sum of money that the publisher is willing to give you to commit to the project and to submit an acceptable manuscript. Once the book is published, the book will start to earn royalties and these will work off the advance (but make sure to confirm this). After the advance is earned, further royalties will be paid if the book sells beyond the amount already advanced you. Most likely, the publisher will not ask for the money back if the book doesn't earn back the advance (ask if the contract doesn't specify it). The publisher will try to give you an amount they feel comfortable the book will earn in its first one or two years. This may be the only money you ever see from the book. Many books in the trade arena never earn back their advance.

There may be items the publisher may charge back to the author's royalties. Examples may include an index, permissions fees to use copyrighted material, illustration costs, and other items. Make sure it is completely spelled out as to who is responsible for what items.

You will probably be paid your royalties once a year. If possible, ask for them to be paid twice a year. Also, if you are to receive an advance for writing the book, the contract should specify when it will be paid (for example, upon contract signing, at manuscript submission).

You've Got Rights, Lefts

The contract will contain details like who owns the copyright and publishing rights to the book. The copyright states who created the material. Copyright exists when the material can be shown to have first been created. Copyright is later registered with the Library of Congress. The copyright for the book may be registered under the publisher's name or under the name of the author. The publishing rights, however, will need to be signed over to the publisher. This gives them the right to make the material commercially available. The publisher will obviously need these rights to make your material available to its customers. Someday when the work goes out of print (hopefully years from now), all rights will revert back to you from the publisher. Make sure this is specified in the contract.

Another area the contract covers and an asset of the book is the rights or subsidiary rights. This means other applications or forms of your work. This may include a paperback version (if the contract is for a hard cover book), film/television/dramatic rights, audio rights, first serial rights (having excerpts run in a magazine before publication), second serial rights (excerpts running after publication), book club rights, electronic rights, or international translation rights (to create foreign language versions).

The contract will specify who holds these rights and how money from these rights will be divided. For instance, the publisher may hold rights to translate the book into a foreign language. It may negotiate with a third party to translate the book into Spanish for a $2,000 fee. You may receive 50% of this payment, and the publisher keeps the rest.

If you have an agent, it may be worthwhile to try to retain some of these rights for him or her to negotiate. Some publishers may not agree, specifically for first-time authors.

What to Negotiate

If you feel the urge to negotiate with the publisher, ask about items that will benefit the book. Sure you can try to get a bigger chunk of money, but when it gets down to firm requests, ask for things that will help the book and therefore benefit you in the long run. Here are some examples:

- Ask whether additional marketing and sales efforts can be made on the book's behalf.
- Ask to have expenses reimbursed. Sometimes publishers will more quickly embrace expenses such as postage, copying, etc, rather than just larger flat sums.
- Ask about including the right to review and/or approve the editing, cover, marketing copy, and promotional pieces (none of which you are guaranteed to be consulted on). Many publishers will reject your requests, while others might make the wording less strident but still amenable. At a minimum your requests will alert the publisher to your interest in being involved with these tasks.
- Ask for more free copies, a greater discount on the ones you can buy after the book is out, or a greater discount on copies you might be purchasing prior to release.
- Ask for the publisher to pay for the illustrations or materials taken from other sources.
- If the book is ever sold at very, very low cost before it goes out of print (called remaindering), then ask to have the first option to buy it at the deeply discounted price.
- Ask to have the contract specify when the book will be released. A common way of expressing it is that 12 or 18 months after the manuscript is accepted, the publisher will agree to have a final book, or the rights revert back to the author.
- Make sure your contract details the physical specifications of your book. If you think it is a big, hard cover glossy text with photos, and the publisher thinks it is a paperback with just text, there is a problem. If it does not specify it, ask for it to be added. If the publisher won't commit to it, ask at least what plans it has so you can flush out any potential misunderstandings.
- The contract may specify something called a reserve for return. This is an amount held back for years to offset returns between royalty statements. Ask to have this eliminated or reduced.

- Ask to have royalties paid more frequently. If they suggest yearly, ask for twice a year. If they offer twice a year, ask for four times a year.
- Sometimes publishers will pay a lower percentage for books sold in great quantity. This is under the idea that the big discount they give should affect both of you. Ask to have this struck from the contract.
- Make sure the contract specifies what geographic region and form the publishing rights cover (for example, world-wide or just North America, all forms or just print rights). If it does not, think about what is in your best interest and have them specified.

Of course, if you have an agent, he or she should hold your hand through the process, negotiating for you on the points he or she knows will be flexible. You will not get everything, but it does not hurt to ask.

If you were taking notes...

1. Your book contract is an important, final step to cement the relationship between you and the publisher.
2. You will need to carefully review and understand each and every point in the contracts. When in doubt, ask the publisher for explanations.
3. The contract will specify exactly how you will be paid with advances and/or royalties.

14

You're Going to be Published!

It's Definite

You have a publisher and perhaps an agent. You have reviewed and signed your contract. You have a deadline for when the manuscript is due, as well as a target release date for the book. Now what?

You have accomplished one of the most difficult parts of the whole process by creating a proposal, finding a publisher and agent, and getting them to say yes. Sure, there is a lot of work left to be done, but these hurdles that you have cleared represent the biggest impediments to the majority of people. Now you have to pony up with the goods. Many aspiring authors would be envious to be in your position.

Review your progress and appreciate your accomplishments. You have rolled the rock to the top of the hill. If you can do that, surely the trip down the hill will be much easier.

Plus, now it is official. You can tell everyone you are writing a book and have a publisher.

HAVING A PLAN

The remaining chapters will discuss the actual process of writing the manuscript. The chapters will talk about getting feedback from your friends and network about the book. Then the next chapters will give an overview of the publication process and the part you will play in it. Finally, the remainder of the book will discuss the all important tasks of marketing and selling your book. Your role in this is crucial to the book's success.

The best way to deal with these steps is to develop a plan, and a timeline for each task. Through seeing this as a journey and not a chore, the process can become faster and more efficient. As you read the next few chapters on manuscript creation, make notes as to how and when you will accomplish each step. Be realistic in your time assessments.

Also, start to keep notes on unique ways in which you might be able to sell your book. Think about connections you have or ways you can let customers know about the book's existence. Spend as much time on marketing as you do on manuscript preparation and writing. Like the tree falling in the forest, if you create and print or publish a book, and no one ever buys it, is it really a book or just a fancy manuscript? Marketing and sales are as important as manuscript creation.

Congratulations on coming this far. The publication of your book is in sight. You might want to also start thinking about what you will do for your second book...

How to Write the Book

15

Creating the Manuscript

Now the Work Starts

Not really. You have done a lot of the important steps already. But there is a very imposing task left—writing the manuscript.

If you have decided to self-publish, you might be picking up here. Or you have an agent and publisher and they actually expect you to send something to them in exchange for that huge advance. The act of actually writing the manuscript can be exhilarating and daunting, but it is just another step toward book publication. You simply need a plan.

Making the Skeleton Come Alive

You have already created a table of contents and a description of the book. You probably also have an outline of each chapter, perhaps sample chapters as well that come from your proposal.

You will need to gradually expand each chapter until you end up with the completed book. Start by taking each chapter title and placing it at the top of a page. Do not worry about getting it exact as the chapter might be split into two or merge with another. This is simply a way to start to organize your material. Add the expanded information from the chapter outline.

Add to each chapter or page roughly three to ten broad points that detail the concepts to be discussed in each. They will probably flow in a logical, sequential order. Some may just be miscellaneous items to be covered in that chapter. Continue to do this for each chapter. When you are done, you will essentially have a list of all the topics you will cover in your book.

Through the process being discussed in this chapter, be open to changing your thinking. This step of adding broad topics to each of your chapters may uncover that some of your chapters are packed while others are sparse. This may lead you to split or combine chapters. Now is the time to do this. Do not wait. Be open to the changes. This step is as much a discovery and educational process for you as it is a writing task.

These broad points or topics can eventually become the headings in your chapters. The headings don't need to be the polished ones, but simply explain what will be covered in the chapter. Once you have this structure, you can start to add other subtopics to the page. Keep adding until you start to exceed a page on each chapter. Then keep expanding the list of items and points. When you start to feel it is becoming a miscellaneous list of items, it is time to write.

This is a Lot of Work

This method of getting started works. However, after you create the extended outline, you might get the feeling that this is a huge task. Well, to be honest, it is a time-consuming task but not an insurmountable one.

You will need to create a schedule for writing. Set aside time each day for you to whittle away at your project. You should leave some days to give yourself a breather. You should also set manageable amounts to be accomplished each day. Be realistic and don't set expectations so high that you will become discouraged if you fall behind.

The length of time it will take to write your manuscript will vary greatly. Factors affecting this include: size of the book you are writing, research to be done, your comfort with writing and revising, your schedule, tasks competing for your time, and your perfectionism quotient.

I would also suggest that as you sit down to start to do the writing, do not start with chapter one. This can feel overwhelming and create a lot of pressure. Write a meat and potatoes chapter toward the beginning or middle of the book. Completing one will give you a sense of accomplishment. If after doing a few of these you want to revisit the first one you did, feel free to revise it. Leave the first chapter until you are in a groove and can sense the tone and tenor of the book.

Research using the library or Internet is an important step as well. You will need to research and verify what information goes into your book. Once a reader starts to find statements that he or she knows not to be true, the reader will start to question everything else as well. Spend the time, do the legwork and get the research done, and do it right the first time. Keep notes on all the facts that you derive from your research so you know where the information came from.

What About That Stuff at the Front and Back of the Book?

You will also need to create the material that runs before chapter one (front matter) and the material that runs after the last chapter (back matter, or sometimes called end matter). The publisher will be responsible for knowing what goes on some of these pages, such as the copyright page and title pages. Here is a brief explanation of the various parts. First the front matter:

- *Testimonials Page:* Starts off the book and will list the endorsements or testimonials you have received. It is more marketing than part of the content of the book.

- *Other Books by the Author:* If this is applicable, maximize this page and list anything that you have done. This is a great marketing opportunity.
- *Title Page:* Lists your title, the publisher, place of publication, and your name. If you have an advanced degree, you can list this here. Also, if it is a technical book, you may want to list your affiliation or place of employment to establish your credibility.
- *Copyright Page:* Lists the standard copyright disclaimer, contact information for the publisher, cataloging information, and Library of Congress data. This is the publisher's responsibility.
- *Dedication:* Your chance to dedicate the work to someone.
- *Table of Contents:* A listing of the chapter titles and other sections or parts of the book, with appropriate page numbers.
- *Acknowledgments:* Your chance to acknowledge the people who helped you with the book. It is okay to list people you have not met, but who still influenced you. Send them a copy of the book. Maybe they will endorse it. Also, do not forget your parents.
- *List of Photographs/Maps/Charts/Illustrations:* Create a list of these items that allows the reader to easily find them in the book.
- *Foreword:* Usually written by someone else, preferably someone famous or influential in your chosen field. It should be an endorsement of you and your book.
- *Preface:* Written by you, it tells why you wrote the book or what inspired you to create it. Use it to establish your credentials.
- *Introduction:* Written by you, it usually tells who you wrote the book for. The introduction also should include the information a reader would need to know about how the book is set up, or any special instructions on how to read or use it.

For the foreword, preface, and the introduction, keep them short. They are not likely to be read and it is better to put the good stuff in the book.

Here are the parts of the back matter:

- *Bibliography or References:* This is the list of materials you used to create your book. There are rules about how to list them. Manuals such as the *Chicago Manual of Style* can help you cite each item correctly.
- *Appendix:* The Appendix is a list of additional materials or documents the reader may find valuable. Think of these resources as bonuses.
- *Glossary:* A short listing of technical terms dealing with the topic of the book. It includes a definition for each term.
- *Index:* A listing of terms from the book with the associated page number. Most times, a publisher will require you to create the index. Most publishers offer the option for a professional indexer to create one for you and charge your royalty. Take this option. Also, make sure the index is a significant length. It is a valuable tool for the reader and some people will use it to decide whether to buy the book or not. It reflects on the quality of the book.
- *About the Author:* This is a version of what you should have used in your proposal. Do not be humble. Make sure you list any other publications you have, as well as anything that qualifies you to write the book. It can run in the front matter or back matter.

Here are some points on other parts of the book:

- *Sections/Chapters:* You will probably separate your book into chapters. There may be larger groupings you would like to separate the chapters into. Review the sections in this book to see how the groupings help the reader understand the major themes in the book.
- *Illustrations:* Your book may have photographs or drawings. They can be essential to your material. They can also become very expensive unless you are able to provide them yourself. You will need to discuss with the publisher who will be responsible for creating them. Also, the majority of photographs or

illustrations in the book may be in black and white. Color, other than on the cover, is very expensive. Exceptions are coffee table books, children's picture books, and some technical works. Finally, the photographs or illustrations are one of many factors that will influence readers to buy (or not to buy) your book. If you are going to have photographs or illustrations, make sure they are top quality. What may be special or cute to you, may not be to others. Avoid relatives and close friends doing the work. Get outside opinions.

- *Permissions:* You may choose to use material from other sources. If you want to use a significant portion, you will need to seek permission from the original source. Please respect the copyright of others and when in doubt, seek permission to use this material. If you are using any material and are unsure if it is permissible, consult with your publisher. Be prepared, there may be a fee. If you do ask for permission from the source, make sure you ask for permission for non-exclusive rights, worldwide, for all formats. If your book sells to an international publisher, you will have secured rights for the item's use. Also, acknowledge all materials that are from other sources with a credit line showing the source.

Editing and Revising

Now that you have the first draft of your book created, you will need to do some editing and revising. Your reaction to this task is probably one of two philosophies. You may be of the type that once something is created and looks passable, you never want to see it again. You may want to get on to the next task or topic. Also, once it is set down on paper, it may feel overwhelming to make substantive changes.

Or you may be of the opposite camp—you love to tinker. Add a comma here, fix a phrase there, add a thought here or there. You may like to tinker so much that it is never final. You may want it perfect, and feel it will never be good enough.

Editing and revising. Love it or hate it, you will need to come to grips with how much you need to do. Avoiding revising completely is just not realistic. It takes a second and third and maybe fourth pass for you to catch what you missed when you created something the first time. If something sounds odd or out of place, it probably will be to your reader as well. Change it. Thinking that perfect prose rolls off your tongue onto the page that needs no corrections is not reality-based. You will need to revise your material to make sure it is as good as it can be.

Conversely, if it is never perfect, and you always need just a little bit more time, you will never have a book. Or you will have an angry agent and publisher. Perfect and flawless is subjective. Your material will need to be looked at by other groups and your publisher. They are more objective, and will be honest over what needs to change as opposed to you obsessively changing the manuscript.

You need to produce a manuscript in a timely fashion, expect revisions, and then you will have a quality product that satisfies every party.

I would suggest putting the manuscript aside for a minimum of a week, or more, to put some distance between you and it. It will give you some perspective on your work.

Also, the editing process is the perfect time to start to get feedback from other people about your work. This will help show you what needs to be worked on most. See the next chapter for advice on how to go about getting this input.

I also like to read aloud anything that I write. First, it refines your speaking skills. Second, it highlights weaknesses in the way some of your thoughts are expressed. As many people have pointed out, the written word is different from the spoken word.

This should be your last opportunity to tinker with the title. It might be fine as is, but once you have a final manuscript you can assess whether the title represents the content, and has enough punch.

Also, I would suggest you keep the various major drafts of the manuscript in paper or electronic form. If you want to go back to a previous version before a rewrite, this will allow you quick access to it. Just keep the latest version clearly marked.

The size of the task of writing your manuscript should not be minimized. It can exceed all the other tasks, or it can be an easier one. It will depend on your circumstances. Also, there are numerous, excellent books on the art and mechanics of writing. Consult them according to your needs and comfort level. These books provide a separate education on a crucial aspect of book publishing.

Finally, there are several schools of thought about writing a book if you do not have a publisher. "Do so at your own risk," or "the effort may prove fruitless." Also, bear in mind that most/all agents and publishers do not require seeing the entire manuscript for non-fiction books.

You are on a roll. You now have two of the key elements in place: a publisher and a final draft manuscript. From here on out things should progress quickly. Having a published book to start to sell to your readers is near. Congratulate yourself on your remarkable headway.

If you were taking notes...

1. Manuscript creation starts with an extensive outline of each chapter. Proceed slowly by expanding each part until the work gradually starts to emerge.
2. You will be responsible for writing the material that comes at the beginning and end of the book, along with obtaining illustrations and permission to use someone else's material.
3. Editing and revising the work will tighten and improve the final manuscript.

16

Getting Your Manuscript Reviewed

Show Me Yours

As you finalize your manuscript, you will need to start to share your work with others. A whole mystique has arisen about this step. Some people are worried about it being bad luck before the manuscript is complete. Or an author may feel self-conscious about putting his or her friends and loved ones in an awkward position of having to say honest things about the work.

You need to start to feel comfortable with the process of sharing your work with others, first in a small circle, and then in an ever-expanding one. Talking about it and sharing it also helps to sharpen your presentation skills, and your own understanding of the material.

I suggest you start to take small increments of the manuscript, perhaps by chapter, and share it with your friends or relatives. If the book is a professional one, sharing it with your colleagues is an important step in checking the quality of the material.

You will gradually get to the point where you will want or need to share the whole manuscript with several people. When you start sharing your material, let people know exactly what you are looking for. Let them know if you would like their general opinion or approval of the material, or whether you want them to only let you know about factual errors, or to check for grammar. Tell them if you would like them to make notes on the manuscript or just give you verbal feedback. Finally, tell them a target time for when you would like their comments returned.

Why Don't You Tell Me What You Really Think

Many people will claim to welcome criticism, however, when it actually shows up they may not embrace it. Criticism, constructive or otherwise, can be very valuable. After receiving it, you need to step away from it being about you or a value judgment on the work. Think about what you can learn from the comments. Positive or negative, there is something for you to take out of everyone's observations.

Think about how your manuscript might be improved by the suggestions you receive. Be willing to step away from it and see it from a different perspective. Many times, authors will get so close to the material that they can miss what could be valuable improvements to the work.

When judging comments that you are on the fence about, it may be worthwhile to bounce the potential improvements off your ideal reader. Picture one solitary person who is the perfect audience for your book. He or she may be a friend or relative, or co-worker. Many authors will write their entire book with this person in mind. If you can come up with a person like this, he or she can be very valuable in the editing or revision process. When you have to decide on whether to incorporate tough comments, you may want to bounce them off your ideal reader. Get his or her opinion on whether the change is for the better, or not.

Consider also giving a preliminary reading to an audience. Take a section of the book or a couple of chapters and do a reading to a potential group of customers. Be open and up front as to what your motives are. Ask for feedback and suggestions. See if they are hungry for more, or whether they think you are missing the mark. Listen closely to what everyone says.

Finally, if you are fortunate to have many people who will read your manuscript, you may start to develop conflicting suggestions. Ones that, while valid, represent a departure from how you wrote the book. These comments may refer to the kind of book that reviewer would like. At some point, you will need to make a judgment call. You have a vision of your book. You have chosen to go down certain roads, while deciding not to go down others. The danger of taking everyone's suggestions is that the book becomes one written by committee. At some point, you will need to stick to your vision and proceed as you see fit.

In addition, receiving lots of similar suggestions from multiple sources may indicate that a chapter (or several chapters) needs reworking. Be open to the possibility that a section needs to be scrapped, and that you may need to rewrite it. While never anyone's favorite choice, this option usually improves a book.

Finally, if your book is of a highly technical nature, it will need to be peer-reviewed, either by you or people selected by the publisher. These individuals will review the work, giving you feedback about your material and what needs to change to represent current thinking on your topic.

Or You Might Need a Professional

Depending on your background and skill set, you may want to consider having a professional give you feedback. The *LMP* lists people and companies that provide editorial services. These companies can be very helpful in increasing the quality of your manuscript. These companies can help with structure or presentation of your thoughts.

This service will obviously cost something. You should know ahead of time exactly what those charges will be. If the company quotes by the hour, ask them for a range of the number of hours that it might take. Do not leave it open-ended. Also, remember that the publisher will be having someone edit it as well. I would only suggest taking this step if you have concerns about your skill level in writing.

If you want to try this, but cannot afford a professional writer or editor, you may want to post a notice at a college looking for an English major. This type of person can be just as helpful, and may charge less. Also, for a student looking for real-life experience, this may be a nice bonus on a future resumé. Or perhaps you know an English teacher at the local high school looking for some extra cash. Either way, do not forget to acknowledge the contribution in the book.

No matter what, look for the finished product to be of great quality that has had independent input from outsiders.

Also, do not forget that anyone who reviews the manuscript can potentially add an endorsement or testimonial to your growing list of people. Whether of eminent stature, or just a neighbor, even quotes such as, "I predict this will be a #1 best-seller—L.M., Langhorne, Pennsylvania," will catch someone's eye.

If you were taking notes...

1. Gradually start to show chapters and your manuscript to friends and colleagues.
2. Be open to all criticism, constructive or otherwise. Learn from it all.
3. You may wish to seek professional help with editing or writing. However, do not duplicate what your publisher will also be doing.

What Happens During the Book Production Process

17

How a Cover is Designed

Judging a Book

Hands down, the cover of your book, along with its title, are the most important elements in a book's success. If you are self-publishing, do not skimp on it and *do not* try to have a friend or relative create it. Get help from a professional.

If a publisher is creating the cover, try to be as involved as you can. Before signing the contract, you may want to discuss your vision of the cover. It will help to verify that you both see eye-to-eye on what the visual representation will be. Some potential authors even have a dummy cover created to submit with their proposal.

Will your cover be a soft focus with muted colors? Will it be bright and eye catching? A photo, or a drawing, or just words? Will it smack you in the face, or catch your attention subtly? Will the words do the talking, or the graphics? These are important aesthetic questions that dramatically affect the way your book is perceived.

Be assured when you are working with cover creation that the old saying about judging the book by its cover exists for a reason. It happens with every book, every day.

I cannot help but add one note. Take a terrible manuscript and give it a great title and great cover, and yes, it will sell better, but it will not last. After being drawn in, people will see it for what it is—junk. Plus it will get bad reviews. Great covers and titles get people to consider the work, but you also have to deliver the goods of great content.

A Beauty Contest

After you determine the feel your cover will have, the next step will be for your publisher to have a designer work up rough versions of the cover. The more designs, the better. In fact, if different designers can create different versions, that is even better, as this will bring different perspectives to the table.

If you have various options, put them up on a wall and absorb them. Do not make an immediate judgment. Have your friends and family give their feedback.

Look at the covers from five to six feet away. Is the title readable? Is the title visible when displayed in black and white? What does it look like when displayed small on a computer screen, as it would at an on-line bookseller?

Cover up the words in the title and ask some people who don't know about the project what they think the book is about. See what message the graphics and design are sending the reader. Ask them how much they think the book costs.

Compare it to the best-sellers in your area of publishing. Make sure that coincidentally you have not matched the design of another book which could lead to confusion, or worse.

Try to judge the design by how professional it looks. Please, please no amateur designs. Please, please no high school yearbook-type collages. The best way to judge the professional nature of a cover is to compare it to the books in a bookstore that are on the best-seller list.

But What Needs to be Included?

The following should be included on your front cover:

- Title and subtitle.
- Author's name(s). Some types of publishing may have you include your degrees, if appropriate. Check what is standard in your area or field.
- Publisher's name (I recommend it go on the front cover, spine and back cover).

The following should be included on your back cover:

- A complete description of the book, written from a marketing perspective. The catchier the better, and with a provocative headline.
- The bar code, ISBN (International Standard Book Number), category to be shelved in the bookstore, and the price.
- Testimonials or endorsements. Use the one(s) with the most punch. If you've got a killer one, perhaps include it on the front cover.
- A brief description of the author's background, to establish you as the expert. Don't be shy. Of course, you will need a great picture of yourself.
- Also, the spine should include the title, author's name, and publisher. They should be very readable from a good distance.

Even if your publisher just gives you the cover and does not ask for feedback, go through these steps anyway. Offer your opinions. Perhaps after they read your comments, some will resonate with the publisher and they may choose to change some of the items.

As with the title, and as with the proposal, spend too much time and too many resources on this part of book. It will be worth it in the long run.

If you were taking notes...

1. The cover is the most important page in the book.
2. Hopefully, several designs will be created to choose from. Get unbiased feedback from friends and strangers.
3. The front and back cover should include specific items. Make sure none are missed.

18

How a Manuscript Becomes a Book

You've Sent It In!

You have sent your final manuscript in to your agent and your publisher. A dynamic cover has been created that you love. The work is done. Well, almost. Before we move on to how a manuscript becomes a book, a couple of points. Make sure you keep a copy of everything that you send in to the publisher. For the manuscript, make sure you keep an electronic and paper copy. Do the same with any images you send them.

Now that the manuscript is with the publisher, you also need to understand that you have ceded control of the manuscript to the publisher. You will *probably* be consulted on changes or alterations. You will *probably* be consulted on the design of the interior of the book. If you go into the process feeling that you have sent your child off to college for new experiences outside your control, than you will be in good shape. Any consultations that the publisher makes with you, if you have this frame of mind, will be a positive experience.

The traditional position has been that since the publisher spends all the money on production, printing, and marketing, it gets to have the final say on these topics. However, make it known to your publisher that you want to be involved in all stages of the book's production. Follow up through the process to ask about the book's progress. Be positive and make sure you let the publisher know you are trying to help improve the quality of the book. Agree with them that they know publishing, but your feedback as an expert in this area will help improve the book's reception with its audience. Through the whole process if you are unsure or do not understand something, ask, ask, ask.

One final note—patience should be the order of the day (or year). Shock of all shocks, the publisher has projects to work on other than yours. Your book will be scheduled for a specific release date or season. The entire schedule works backwards towards its release. Most authors feel it is not quick enough, but you will need to have patience.

Step by Step

When the publisher receives your manuscript, it will be assigned to an editor. This editor may be an employee or a freelancer. It is important to see your editor as an ally, not an adversary. He or she is working on your behalf to make your book a better product.

The manuscript will be reviewed by the editor, publisher, or others to assess whether your work is what they asked you to write. They may be able to make this judgment themselves. Or, if it is of a technical nature, then they may send it through peer review, where it is sent out to other experts in the field for them to offer their judgment.

Assuming the publisher and others find the manuscript acceptable, they will move on to the production process. The editor will start with an initial read-through of the manuscript, making the first edits to your work. Some will do this editing on paper, while others will make the changes directly into the electronic file.

The editor will be checking for grammar, spelling, and punctuation, but also to make sure the material flows logically and clearly. He or she will want to ensure that the reader is getting his or her questions answered by the way you present the material. He or she may start to change or even rewrite sections. How much this is done will depend on the material, your ability, and the publisher and editor.

After the editing process, the next step will be typesetting or page make-up. The book will pass from the publisher to graphic designers or people responsible for making the edited manuscript look like the pages in a book. This process has evolved in just a few years from a complicated one requiring specialized equipment done by someone with a technical background, to one that can be accomplished on almost any computer that has specialized and relatively easy to use software.

Taking One Last Look

The result will be a print out or page proofs of your edited final manuscript. It will look and feel like the real thing. Various publishers may take different steps along the way and require different things from the author as the process progresses. They should spell it out for you so that you are fully aware of what will occur.

The publisher should also give you the opportunity to review your work or the page proofs. Some may send you the edited manuscript before it is converted into pages, and then again in page proof form. Many will send you just page proofs for your review.

This is probably your one and only chance to review the book in its edited and changed form. Set aside the appropriate amount of time to review it based on when the publisher needs the pages returned. Read the manuscript through to see how it has changed. Do not rewrite their changes to put them back the way they were. Ask about any changes or alterations and why the changes were made. Ask in a positive manner; do not make demands.

Note any corrections that need to be made. Keep a copy of the changes you have requested. After the publisher receives your comments, follow up and ask if changes were made, and if you will see another set of pages.

After the changes have been made, the publisher will probably review and re-read the book one more time. Then it is off to the printer.

If possible, get a copy of the final page proofs that the publisher sent to the printer. These pages virtually duplicate what the book will look like, and can be helpful with marketing.

The publisher will give you a target date of when you should be seeing an advanced copy. The only thing left in regard to production is patience—waiting for this date to arrive. The date you receive the first advanced copy is not the official release date. These dates may be separated by days, weeks, or months. The official release date is timed by the publisher to coincide with a selling season or the book's availability to its customers or distributors.

The time waiting for the first copy will be no time to relax. All through the process of manuscript creation, and even prior to that, you will need to have been busy with marketing and publicity.

The next two chapters detail what should happen when selling the book, and most importantly, what role you can play. Marketing is the least understood part of the publishing process by most authors, yet it might just be the most important part of what an author can do to make a book a best-seller.

These activities will all need to be minutely orchestrated to coincide with the book's release. You may be contacting local newspapers or national magazines, setting up interviews, arranging a party or getting a web site created.

All of your efforts—writing, editing, looking at page proofs, beginning marketing and publicity efforts—all lead up to one thing. You are days away from officially being a published author.

If you were taking notes...

1. When you submit your manuscript to your publisher, it will be assigned to an editor who will review it for acceptability, grammar, and style.
2. The publisher will then have it set up in page proof form.
3. You will probably have one last time to review the changes and edits before the book is sent to the printer.

How to Market and Promote Your Book

19

Marketing, Distribution, and Publicity

THIS IS WHAT IT IS ALL ABOUT

To be honest, these next two chapters are the most important in this book. But these chapters also will probably be the least read, least followed, or least understood.

Marketing, sales, promotion, publicity, advertising, distribution. They all run together for most people. These terms, however, serve a separate yet harmonious role in spreading the word about your book. You can play a part in most of them. You should also know exactly what your publisher will do (and not do) in this area. This lets you to know where you may have to put additional efforts.

I have always been amazed that an author can write a 500 page manuscript and spend months revising and doing research on his or her topic. Then, many of these same well-meaning authors will studiously avoid all promotional and marketing duties. Some authors feel they have done their part and this is the publisher's job. Others feel it is below them or unseemly for them to promote their own work. When a book disappears from the radar screen after six months and then it is moved to the discount rack after twelve months, the author should not complain. If you do not want to take as active a role in marketing and promotion as you did in writing, you are missing out on opportunities to make your book a success.

Defined

Here are some of the terms that may be the cause of some confusion to the novice:

- *Promotion:* Refers to letting your customers know about the book. It is a broad term that covers many types of activities. Most times, these efforts are time intensive and cost you little or nothing.
- *Publicity:* Refers to the result of promotion when the media (and customers, depending on the context) find out about your book, with the result being exposure to readers, listeners, etc. Most times, these efforts have had little to no cost, but can have a high payoff when done effectively.
- *Advertising:* This usually refers to placing an advertisement in a magazine, newspaper, newsletter, etc. The ad may be paid for, or be provided in exchange for some service or other arrangement. The desired result will be for the customer to buy the book, go to the bookstore, or possibly attend your speaking engagement (where the customer will buy the book).
- *Marketing:* A broad term that covers all of the formal activities of letting people know about the book. This may include writing the descriptive copy for the book, creating a direct mail piece, dealing with distributors/bookstores/libraries, etc.
- *Sales:* This term refers to actually talking to customers about your book. It may mean just one customer at a presentation you are giving, or talking to a bookstore manager, or to a company that may buy the book in quantity. It means convincing one person that the book is right for his or her needs.

- *Distribution:* Refers to getting your books to companies that will put them in the hands of potential customers. These middlemen may distribute your book to bookstores, libraries, specialty stores, or other retail outlets. This group may include distributors or wholesalers; they may be exclusive or not; and they may be regional, national, or international.

No matter which term, the goal of all of them is to get books in the hands of potential customers.

Markets, Markets, Markets

One of the first things that you should have concentrated on, way back at the proposal stage, was your market. What is the profile of people who will want to buy the book? What is their typical age? Gender? Educational background?

Do they belong to any specific organizations or clubs? Do they subscribe to any special magazines? Work in specific locations? The more you formulate in your mind who your potential readers or customers are, the easier promoting and marketing your book will be.

Try to talk with some people who fit the demographics of your readers with whom you are not already acquainted. Ask them what magazines they subscribe to. Where do they hear about new books? How do they find out new information about their hobby or the topic of your book? Do they go to bookstores? Have they ever bought a book at some place other than a bookstore?

Defining your ideal market and customer will be the key to all future successful efforts.

Who Does What

You should have a clear idea of exactly what the publisher will be doing for your book, and what you will or can do to help. Hopefully, early on in the process (at contract signing time) you discussed with the publisher what they will commit to. Perhaps you even got the publisher to put it in writing.

It is (fortunately or unfortunately) part of the system, that the author will help with the publicity and promotion of the book. Many times authors are amazed to find out about this expectation. The feeling I have heard sometimes is, "Geez, I wrote the book, and now I have to help sell it, too?" This feeling is part of what plays into some people's interest in self-publishing.

Like it or not, it is part of the system. That is why having a clear understanding on your part and the publisher's part will save problems later.

Even with this understanding, the publisher may change their commitment. As sales improve, it may do more. Conversely, if sales do not meet its expectations, it may withdraw promised efforts. It is basing many decisions on its entire line of books, not on just one. In any case, have a clear idea of responsibilities ahead of time.

A face-to-face meeting with the publisher about the book in general or just on the topic of marketing is the ideal. This will allow your enthusiasm to spill over. It will allow you the opportunity to personalize your connection with the people who will be working on your book, and to assess their commitment. If this is not feasible, telephone calls will have to suffice. Personal calls are essential. Don't settle for trying to do this by email or letter.

Hopefully, you have a handle on the fundamentals of marketing, distribution, and promotion. You have determined that you are going to work with the publisher as partners to sell lots of books. Now let's talk about specific efforts.

If you were taking notes...

1. Promotion, publicity, advertising, marketing, sales, and distribution are related terms all with the same goal of letting people know about your book and getting them to buy it.
2. Knowing your market and how to reach readers within that market is the key to all efforts.
3. Make sure you have discussed with your publisher who is responsible for which efforts and how much it will commit to.

20

Selling and Promoting Books

What Will the Publisher Do?

Let's look at what the publisher might do for your book and what you might do to help promote and market your book. *The actual list will vary greatly from book to book, from topic to topic, and from publisher to publisher.* For example, some topics are very suited to direct mail, while others will be sold primarily through ads. You will need to adapt these options to your individual circumstances. If your publisher is not using one of these methods that does not automatically mean the publisher is doing a bad job.

The publisher *may* be responsible for:

- Making the book available in bookstores, whether they are the big chain bookstores or independent ones. The publisher will use a distributor to get the books into the stores. Its distributor may just take orders, or the distributor may actively promote the book. The distributor may call on all stores, or just certain types or ones in a geographic area. If your book is a specialized or technical one, it is more important that the publisher have the book in technical bookstores, as opposed to bookstores at a mall. Beware, returns of unsold books plague the industry. Books that are "sold" to a bookstore can easily be returned. This is true for other avenues as well, but not to the degree as with a bookstore. Representation in chain or independent bookstores many times is the yardstick by which authors measure success. However, these sales can be some of the most difficult and problematic.

- Selling the book to libraries. The publisher will use a specialized distributor, a library distributor, to get the word out. Libraries are a great place to have your book and expose it to readers. Some of these customers will eventually buy the book for themselves. Plus, if your book is worn because of use, the library may repurchase a copy or copies.
- Contacting retail outlets other than bookstores about your book. These locations can be some of the best, and most lucrative options. Did you write a cookbook? Sell it at restaurants or specialty food stores. A book on collectible dishes? How about trying to sell it in antique stores? A book on vacationing in your town or state? How about selling it to the chamber of commerce or bed and breakfasts? There has been a growing trend to sell more and more books in these varied locations, most of which will not return unsold books.
- Having a toll-free number, or at least a regular phone number, that customers can call to order the book, if not 24 hours a day, then the better part of the day. If the publisher has one, make sure you memorize it and are able to give it to anyone on a moment's notice. List it on all the correspondence or fliers for the book.
- Having a web site and a specific web page for your book. The book should be able to be purchased on-line with a credit card. You should be able to have a specific web address to give out to anyone. It should be simple. For instance, *www.youcanwrite-andpublish.com* is a web address that is easy to remember. If the address is long, contains your ISBN or book number, or codes

like "html", you should rethink it and come up with a better one.

- Making the book available through the major on-line bookstores, like amazon.com, barnesandnoble.com, and others. The book should be a stocked item and should be available for quick delivery. The publisher or its distributor needs to be on good terms with these influential outlets. Also, all the information the publisher presents on your book needs to be comprehensive, complete and include all favorable reviews. Also, as a side note, the publisher or you need to make sure your book is being picked up and indexed by all the major search engines.
- Making copies of the book available at your speeches. These copies can fly off the table at successful speaking events. "Back of room sales" can be an important arrangement to have the publisher involved in. The books would need to be transported to the talk, sold, and the leftover books and receipts returned to the publisher (or you). These arrangements need to be executed flawlessly. If books arrive on Wednesday after your Tuesday presentation, the opportunity is lost.
- Making fliers available to you for any presentations or talks you are giving. The flier should have a description, copy of the cover, and complete ordering information (web site, phone number, address, fax number). The flier should also have a promotional code that can be tracked to see how many people order off of it. Sometimes your flier might have "additional books of interest" done by your publisher by other authors. Make sure you ask if yours, in turn, can be included on other books with a similar audience.
- Providing a copy to appropriate magazines, newspapers, and newsletters for review. These copies are sent free and may be sent out prior to the book being released. These media outlets are some of the best sources of publicity for the book. Since most books are very cheap to print, there should be no skimping on this low cost, high results promotion. A letter with appropriate bibliographic and ordering information should be included with the book.

- Contacting magazines, newspapers, or web sites (some of the very same ones in the item above) about possibly publishing a story that involves the topic of the book. If you wrote a book about snowboarding, perhaps contact the winter sports magazines with an article on the "7 Top Tips for Buying a Snowboard." Of course, your article, and the blurb at the end, would reference the book and how to order it. Plus, you might get paid to write the article.
- Possibly arranging for radio or television interviews. For many people, this is the Holy Grail. It is a realistic consideration for some topic areas, and not even in the realm of possibility for others. Talk to your publisher to honestly assess your chances here. Perhaps your opportunities are limited to your local media outlets, with the angle being that a local person wrote a book. Even this works. *Essential* to any interview is to have the books in the bookstores. If the customer goes to the bookstore to look for it and cannot find it, he or she probably won't come back. This is when a catchy web site address will come in handy. However, do not rely on it, as some people still won't buy a book on the web.
- Possibly creating a press kit, which would include a press release about your book, a picture of the front cover, a ready made story for someone to run about the topic of the book, perhaps a picture of you, and some frequently asked questions and answers. These press kits are great to provide to radio or TV stations, or to potential interviewers.
- Providing sales support to professors to make them aware of the book if the book might be used in a college course. When a course uses a book, it is called an adoption of that text. Most commonly, the instructor is given a free copy of the book. Once again, skimping in this area (if the book has a legitimate audience here) is foolhardy as this is can be a low cost, high return effort.
- Creating a flier or direct mail piece to be mailed to a very focused, targeted list of potential customers. For certain topics in certain areas, this can be very successful. For many others,

however, it can be disastrously expensive. If you wrote a general cookbook, it will be very difficult to make money mailing it to all potential customers. If you wrote a cookbook based around American Revolution recipes, then sending a direct mail piece to the Daughters of the American Revolution might work.

- Including the book in the publisher's seasonal or yearly catalog. This catalog will be used in several ways, such as sending out to its distributors or best customers. Try to make sure your book is given a good position in the catalog. Beware, paper catalogs are on their way to becoming dinosaurs because of printing costs and the exciting electronic options.
- Including your book in catalogs by other companies who sell products similar to yours. If you have a book on how to become an historical re-enactor, then perhaps it would be successful in some of the catalogs (or web sites) that sell the items to these re-enactors. Most likely it will take detective work on your part to find some of the ones more tailored to your individual topic. Do the work yourself and have the publisher make the contact.
- Creating an email campaign to the publisher's best customers to let them know about the book. Perhaps it can offer a 10% off pre-publication discount to develop pre-orders. Or the publisher could rent email addresses for a very focused group. Unfortunately, with the explosion of junk email, or spam, this avenue of promotion has dropped in importance and effectiveness.
- Creating an advertisement to run in a magazine, newspaper, or newsletter about the book. This is extremely rare because of the economics. Selling $25 books one at a time via an ad is tough. If you are writing in a specialized market, there might be specialty or trade publications that work, but this is doubtful. Some people have been successful by trading books or a story for a free ad placement. Others have said that a small magazine might run an ad for a reduced price and a cut of the sales. These options in today's business climate are much less likely, unless the magazine is a one-person operation and you have a relationship with the magazine's publisher.

- Pursuing special sales to companies or non-retail outlets. Let's say you wrote a book on the history of the wine cork. Approaching wine manufacturers would make sense. They might wish to give them to their distributors or customers, stock them in their stores or catalog, or give a copy away to anyone who buys a case of wine. If you wrote a book on how to do different skateboard tricks, why not contact some skateboard manufacturers? These sales, while a challenge to obtain, can be highly lucrative and instantly put your book in the publisher's best-seller category. Think creatively and give a list of possible companies to your publisher for it to pursue. Also, don't forget associations or clubs. Did you write a book on your Italian heritage? How about approaching the Sons of Italy?
- Preparing a plan for possible seasonal tie-ins. Think of natural times of year or holidays that may be a reason for additional efforts. Timing is key. If you have a book about the United States flag, Flag Day and July 4th are givens. But the publisher or you will need to plan these nine to twelve months in advance for many media outlets to coordinate promotional and sales efforts.
- Perhaps making the book available internationally. This will vary greatly from publisher to publisher, and market to market. Many books have little market outside the United States. Some publishers and authors will want to serve these markets directly by selling to them, others will want an exclusive distributor in that area to resell them, while many will want to sell the rights there and have that publisher sell a local version (and simply receive the revenue for the sale). Either way, discuss with your publisher if your book will be available outside the United States and ask for the details of that process.
- Pursuing the rights sales I have previously discussed. Perhaps a book club edition, or maybe an excerpt running in a national magazine. Your publisher or agent may be responsible for this step.

To reiterate, *no publisher* will do all of these items on every or any book. Most times, the individual market will dictate what is accepted practice. If you write a technical book for nurses, you will probably not have any radio interviews. Likewise, if you write a small paperback book of local jokes, a direct mail piece will probably not be profitable. It is best to talk with your publisher and find out what it will be doing *and not doing* in these areas.

WHAT CAN THE AUTHOR DO?

You have your final manuscript done, and now you want to turn your attention toward letting people know about it. You are sold on the importance of marketing and promotion. *Remember, all of these activities will not fit all topics*. Here is a list of some activities that might be appropriate for your area:

- The number one goal is to expose the book to people who will have a fairly high level of interest about it. Whether accomplished through talks, or writing articles, or interviews, or meeting bookstore managers, it comes down to personal efforts. Think of who might be interested in your book and think about where those people can be found.
- Speak to groups, big and small, and diverse. Find local organizations, clubs, or civic groups that might be receptive to your book. Is it a professional book? Speak at as many regional and national meetings as you can. Refine your speech. Make it one that people will remember and one that they would refer to other groups. After you speak, ask the group if they can suggest any other groups that they are a member of that might enjoy your speech. Whatever you do, speak, speak, speak. Make people know about and become interested in you and your book. There are speakers bureaus (see *LMP*). See about being listed with them. Need to refine your speaking abilities? There is a great group with many local chapters called Toastmasters. See the Appendix for contact information. A side note: after the book is published keep a copy to make notes in after each

speech. When a listener asks you questions or makes comments, this is the best way to start to prepare for a second edition.

- Try to arrange for yourself, or through your publisher, to do book signings at your local bookstore. Sign books and revel in the spotlight. Try to make your time at the bookstore a talk on the topic of your book, more than a signing. Would you rather have me sign your book, or go to a talk on how you can write a book? An important note for book signings or talks: take a back-up copy of everything. A box of books, a poster, fliers, pens, maybe even a portable microphone. Like the Boy Scouts say, "Be Prepared." Assume that what can go wrong, will. You will be happy you did. Bring business cards and bookmarks that have your order information. Business cards will help people remember the title of the book, or they can use it to write you a note. Leave a sign-up sheet for people to get on your mailing list. Send people fliers about the book.
- Speak at libraries and make friends with librarians. Most medium- or large-sized libraries will allow you to present to their patrons. Many will allow you to sell books afterwards. Give a talk on the topic of your book. Also, get to know the librarians and find out about the systems of which they are members. Regional library systems can have significant buying power and getting to know the person responsible at the main office (either in person or by sending a free book) can lead to good things in regard to sales and publicity. Whether speaking at bookstores, libraries, or other groups, make sure these engagements are well-advertised and therefore well-attended.
- Get as much media coverage (local, regional, or national) as you can get. When the book is about to be released, contact all the local newspapers and media outlets. Let them know about the book, and that a home town boy (or girl) made good. Local newspapers love these stories. Make sure the newspapers run the contact information on how to order the book. Ruthlessly follow up on this. The editors understand why you will follow up on this. Nothing will dishearten you more than you getting a clip-

ping of a great story about the book where there is no contact information or the title is wrong! Newspapers, newsletters, magazines, web sites, radio stations, and other mediums are constantly faced with filling pages on time. Newspapers and magazines welcome a creative, unique story that is basically finished. Don't ask them to promote your book, tell them you have a great story idea and get them excited about it. If the story will be in interview form, be prepared to explain your book in three sentences, five maximum. The simpler the better. During the interview, refer to your book by title at least three times.

- Have your own web site, preferably using your name. The site can be simple, containing information about you, the book, a sample chapter, the table of contents, a way to contact you, and information about your speeches and presentations. Of course you will want a way to sell the book on-line. The more free material connected to your topic that you can post at your site, the more likely it is customers will return and perhaps buy. Perhaps link the customer to your publisher's web site to make the purchase, or better yet, list links to the on-line bookstores that support you the most (for example, amazon.com or barnesand noble.com). If your name is taken as URL (for example my name, John Bond, was taken), then try something else, like www.booksbyjohnbond.com. Maintain the site yourself (or have a service do it for you). This becomes a place to send potential customers or people to book you for a speaking engagement. Also, if you write books with different publishers, they can all be housed under this one site that you can refer a customer to.
- Mention your book in all your communications. When you email someone, have your automatic signature include the book title and web site address. For instance:

  John Bond
  Author of *You Can Write and Publish a Book*
  www.booksbyjohnbond.com

  This allows you to remind everyone about your book each time they receive an email from you. You can do this with letters and faxes as well.

- Join listserves in your area of expertise. Join in the discussion, and quote your book if appropriate. Important note: check whether it is acceptable to mention or discuss your product before doing so. For some lists, this is a big no-no.
- Create a blog. This exploding phenomena has caught fire in many areas. A blog, for the remaining few that have not heard the term yet, is short for web log. It is a web site that contains a journal of your thoughts or contributions. People are able to visit and, depending on what is permitted, read or comment on your observations. In the political arena and some entertainment areas, blogs have developed into the next big thing. Search your topic in a place like Google to see if there is a dominant blog or if the number is rapidly expanding. As with any web site, you will need to have readers/people/customers come to it and interact with it. If not, you run the risk of being the tree falling in the woods. See how you can position this to directly tie into your book and help with its promotion.
- Free books, while an expense, can be a tremendous marketing tool. A free copy sent to a bookstore manager, editor of a newspaper, a key person in your field, or to a distribution contact can make all the difference in the world. Maybe your book unit cost is $2.50 and shipping and an envelope adds another $1.50 or so. If your publisher is being stingy, let them know. Or if the prospect is very promising, send it yourself.
- Give your book away. Whenever there is a chance to raffle or donate your book to a good cause or charity, please do so. Ask the people running the raffle or auction to display fliers next to it. If there is a program, ask that the book title and web site address be listed.
- Use those quotes. You worked awfully hard on those endorsements. Hopefully you got some more once the book was published. Also, reviews might be coming in from various publications. Put them to maximum use. Here are some examples: display them on your web site, create a sheet of the best ones to be displayed at your talks or signings, quote them in any letters you

send out about the book, add the best one to your email signature, add them to amazon.com and barnesandnoble.com web sites, or innumerable other creative ways.

- Have a party. Invite five to ten diverse creative friends or acquaintances. Feed them dinner and let them have a few drinks. Tell them about how books are sold and what you and your publisher are doing. Have them brainstorm ways to sell the books. Can they suggest groups to talk to? Associations or companies that might want to buy the book? Do they know famous people who might want to write an endorsement? Can they think of unique or quirky ways to promote the book to your target audience? Listen and let the ideas flow. Many ideas will be too expensive, but undoubtedly some good ones will emerge.
- Take a vacation. Your publisher may have an annual sales meeting where all the sales people who call on bookstores get together to hear about new products. It might be in a nice place like Florida or California. Ask if you can stop by (at your expense). They probably won't let you spend a lot of time speaking to the group, but offer to stop by and meet them during coffee breaks or a cocktail party. Be prepared to give your five sentence pitch on why your book is the best thing going, and then answer any of their questions. If you get them excited about the book, it will help with sales. However, be realistic that the publisher has a lot of other projects it is selling as well. Also, every time you take a vacation after that, you might want to devote a half a day to doing a couple of bookstore signings. Increase your exposure in that part of the country. Check with your accountant, because part of the trip (as many of your other expenses as an author) may be tax deductible.
- Sell your book one book at a time. In bookstores it is called handselling. Get one person excited about a book and if he or she likes it, he or she will tell others. Some of the most famous self-published works began with an author with a vision that spoke to anyone who would listen about the book. The author would drive from place to place with a trunk full of books, and

started a revolution. You can make the difference. You are the spark. The publisher can only help fan the flames.

Create a Marketing and Promotion Plan for your part. List the items you know you can do and others you would like to attempt. List them by category, with all of the ones dealing with speaking together, and so on. Later, you can create a timeline of what needs to occur when. This plan is a living, breathing document that will change as time progresses. Keep it by your bedside or on your desk. It will be your road map to success.

Be aware that many of these items start well before manuscript submission. Some can continue to occur well after publication. They need to be carefully timed for maximum effectiveness.

Also, there are many, many good marketing books about on-line marketing, and how to get publicity. Some are listed in the Bibliography, or you can go to an on-line bookstore and search.

What to Ask

Having read all of the possible activities a publisher might do for your project, here is a list of questions to ask before you start to work together. There are no right or preferred responses. What is right for your book will depend on the publisher and the market. Do not be afraid to ask or make requests of the publisher. Unfortunately, the publisher has a lot to do, but the squeaky wheel does get the oil.

Bearing in mind the bulleted items above, here are some questions to ask:

1. Will my book be in most bookstores? Does your sales force call on most stores? On the chain stores?
2. How will you let libraries know about my book?
3. Do you have a web site? Will customers be able to order the book on-line? Will it be considered an in-stock item at on-line stores like amazon.com?
4. Will you be able to provide fliers for me for my own promotional efforts? Is there a limit to the number of copies that I can have?

5. What support can you give me as I try to arrange speaking engagements?
6. Is there a phone number where the book can be ordered? Is it staffed 24 hours a day?
7. What are your general guidelines on complimentary review copies? How many can I expect to be sent out to magazines and newspapers?
8. How will my book and the other titles you publish be marketed together? Will each of our books benefit from the other's efforts?
9. Will it be available outside the United States? How and through whom? Will your editors try to sell the rights to publishers outside the United States? Or should my agent do this?
10. Do you have close contacts with any media outlets where you can discuss possible coverage when the book is released? How can I help?
11. What kind of effort will you have in regard to special sales for my book in bulk?
12. When will marketing and promotional efforts start prior to the book's release? How long after its release will it continue to receive active attention?
13. Will I be able to give you feedback about the marketing materials that you create for my book?

Slavishly devote yourself to promoting and marketing the book. Do it long after the publisher has moved on. Spend more time implementing the ideas in these chapters than you spent on creating the rest of the book.

Work at promotion like this is what makes or breaks the book, because it will. If you worry that your book will end up being unknown and not bought by anyone, your efforts in this area can help prevent this.

Try to do one thing each day or seven things a week to let people know about your book. Develop a love of speaking about your book and selling it.

If you were taking notes...

1. The publisher should have multiple efforts to spread the word about the book and to sell copies. The list in this chapter includes some of the common ones.
2. You can help in many ways with additional or complimentary activities that promote the book. The list in this chapter includes some of the helpful ones.
3. A list of questions to pose to the publisher is included. The answers should help define roles in promotion.

Section VII

Additional Tasks if Self-Publishing

21

What Self-Publishers Need to Do

Doing More

If you are self-publishing, your efforts to this point would have included all of the items previously discussed. Since you are writer, editor, publisher, marketer, publicist, and warehouse clerk (unless you choose to pay someone to take on some of these tasks), you will need a comprehensive plan to make sure all the balls that you need to juggle stay in the air.

Most of these tasks cannot be done sequentially; that is write the manuscript, *then* arrange for a distributor, *then* set up your company and so on. They will need to be done in concert with each other, or simultaneously. Start to make lists of the different tasks that need to happen. As these lists emerge, start to arrange them in chronological order and assign target dates.

There are some excellent books that take the budding self-publisher from soup to nuts. These books address many of the business matters that need not be addressed in this book. I suggest you find these books (listed in the Bibliography), buy them, and implement the suggestions applicable to you. These books will guide you through the process. And as previously mentioned, there are some lively listserves that generate a tremendous amount of information about publishing that will be a big help to self-publishers. Sign up today!

If you are publishing your book with a publisher, this chapter has less applicability to you, but you also might learn a thing or two if you do read it.

What I Need to Do That Others Don't

Listed below are some points that you will need to start to concern yourself with. These tasks would *not* need to be done by someone publishing a book by the traditional route. More details about them are available in other books strictly on self-publishing:

- Create a company and/or incorporate. Even if you are publishing your book through some of the print-on-demand companies, there may still be benefits to incorporating or creating a similar legal entity that may help with tax or liability issues. Consult an attorney, your accountant, or the Small Business Administration for what works best for you. Finally, when and if you create a company name, please make it a big league name. Keep your name and initials or your town and street name out of it. Think big.
- Copyright the book, get an International Standard Book Number (ISBN), get the Library of Congress information for your book, and other tasks to establish your book and company as legitimate entities.
- Determine whether you want to have publisher's liability insurance. This insurance can protect you against frivolous lawsuits.
- Establish relationships with book distributors and wholesalers. This means that you will need to generate excitement on their part for your book and the accompanying promotional efforts.
- Establish a way to process orders and ship books. You may outsource this task or you may wish to do this yourself at home.

Will you be able to process credit cards? Have a telephone number where books can be ordered? Have a web site and take orders off of it? Where will the books be stored? Do you have a commercial bank account?

- Find a printer that you would feel comfortable working with. Start to get an idea of who would print the book and how much it would cost.

What I Need to Do Differently From Others

There are several tasks that you will still need to coordinate if you are self-publishing (which may seem more geared toward publishing) or that you will need to do differently. Here are a few:

- As mentioned, I encourage you to write a proposal. This will help you focus on what your book is about. It will also be very useful in regard to writing your marketing copy and other promotional tasks.
- You will still need to get endorsements from experts in your field, but you can wait until the manuscript is a draft or in a completed stage. It is not necessary to have them done at proposal stage as you have already convinced the publisher (you!) to publish the work. It is just as important, if not more so, to get great endorsements to help sell the book. You are the little guy and need to overcome the competition.
- I would still examine the *LMP* very closely. Although you are not looking for an agent or publisher, it contains a wealth of marketing and distribution contacts. Also, they list many companies whose services you might need, such as editorial services.
- You will still need to edit your work, but you may need outside help. You may want to enlist the services of a professional, who is unbiased about the book's quality.

- As mentioned before, *do not* skimp on the cover design. Get it done right. Spend money. For the measly dollars that need to be spent, have your cover rival Random House's.
- Marketing, marketing, marketing, marketing. You are smaller. You will need to work harder and smarter than the traditional publishers. You will need to make every hour spent promoting the book and every dollar spent be more focused and more effective. And there will be a lot more fun.

You are off to the races at this point. Enjoy your efforts and bask in each order, no matter how big or small the check. Also, remember, do not let a day or week go by without doing something to spread the word about the book.

If you were taking notes...

1. Self-publishers will need a plan and a timeline to accomplish the many additional tasks they need to do in order to have their book come to fruition.
2. There are several business and distribution tasks that will need to be started and worked on concurrently as you create your manuscript.
3. Some tasks that apply to both self-publishers and mainstream published authors will need to have additional or supplemental focus.

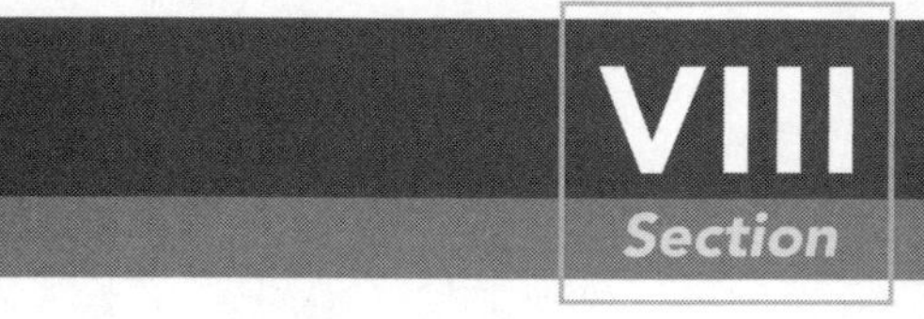

The End of the Road

22

Congratulations!

It's Here

The UPS delivery person knocks at the door. This is the payoff—the moment of truth. You rip open the box. There it is. It is even better than you imagined. *Now* it is official. You are a published author.

You have been working to set up speaking engagements about the book. You have interviews lined up with local newspapers. Your web site has launched and some people actually visited it (other than you).

The publisher's promotional efforts are underway. Books are now on the way to the bookstores. The distributors are excited about the book. They are spreading the word.

You can just hear the sales being rung up and the royalties being calculated. Enjoy this moment. Make the best of it, because there is still a lot to be done.

Your To Do List

Think of today as January 1st. A new year has begun. A new chapter in your life, as you are now a published author. Here is your list of the *Lucky Eleven Things To Do:*

1. Take one day for yourself. Relax. Call your friends and family and tell them the news. Brag, but in a nice way. Put your feet up. Enjoy the day, as there is a long and fulfilling road ahead.

2. Make a resolution to use this new aspect of your life to its fullest. When you send emails, use the book and its web site as your email signature. Mention it to new people you meet. Talk about it in your speeches. Carry it with you wherever you go. Give copies as gifts.

3. Realize that you are an expert. Book publication confers status upon you. How much you believe you are an expert will subconsciously be transmitted to others. Use this elevation in a positive, productive way.

4. Give yourself a party. Whether you call it a book signing, or a launch party, or something else, it will help spread the word about the book. Perhaps you can get publicity for the party. Make it all work for you.

5. Retake the Self-Assessment Quiz from Chapter 2 and see what has changed. You have probably learned a lot. Your score has also changed and now you can see just how far you have come.

6. Remember that marketing and promotion need to be happening all the time. Make a vow to not become complacent. Stay in touch with the publisher over what you are doing, and more importantly, what they are doing. Right after publication, you may need to stay in touch every other day or thereabouts. After a while, continue to talk to the publisher, perhaps once a week.

7. Stick to the Marketing and Promotion Plan that you created. Add items or alter others as things evolve. You should continue to consult the plan and add to it as time goes on.

8. Start a campaign to add to your testimonials and endorsements. Now that your work has become an actuality, more people will probably be willing to look at the book. Ask people who said no already, or people who did not answer. Now you can start your letter, "You may have seen my recently published book..." These new blurbs can be added to future printings of the book, or to your web site, or to promotional materials. Think big and do not be afraid to ask, especially since you are a published author.
9. Speak, speak, speak. Find groups that are appropriate to your area and talk to them. Display books or fliers. Take every opportunity to talk about the book.
10. Send copies of the book to influential people in the field. Of course, you can ask them for an endorsement, but also to let them know the book exists. Ask them if they have any suggestions for spreading the word about the book. They may even end up mentioning it to some other important people as well.
11. See your new accomplishment as a fundamental change in your background. You have a new career (or part-time career). Adjust your thinking and priorities as such.

Congratulations on your hard work and perseverance. You should be proud of your accomplishment. Whether it has to do with marketing or possibly keeping the book up-to-date via a new edition, think of the process as one that does not end. It is not a 50-yard dash. It is not even a marathon. Think of it as a life-long commitment. If done right, the package that you just received should not be a blip on a radar screen. It should continue to reverberate for years to come.

23

Now Do it All Over Again

The First Time Is Always the Most Difficult

A common response by first-time authors to a book's publication is relief. Their lives may have been put on hold. They may have even become sick of the subject they were writing about. Thinking about writing and publishing *another* project right after their book came out would be out of the question. Besides, they might say, "I have all that marketing to do."

Other people, however, may be energized by the book's publication and immediately want to move on to a new project. Either way, as you work on marketing the first project, I suggest you start to think about what other book you might be interested in writing.

The *second* book you work on will be easier. You have invented the wheel and understand the process so much more. Many of the errors you could make have already been made. Think of your first project as the guinea pig. Remember, you are now an expert, not only in your field, but in publishing. Okay, maybe not an expert in publishing, but you are more of a veteran than most everyone you know.

When thinking about a second project, consider quite a bit of the road already hoed. Perhaps use the same agent, publisher, or promotional efforts. Some new topics may require changes, some may not. If you have gone from traditional herb gardening to cooking with herbs, then your current publisher may not serve both markets as effectively.

When you are thinking about a second project, I suggest you think of one that will compliment your first book, or at least sell nicely next to it. Think of your readers and what they may want to buy together. I would not suggest your book be a "II." If you wrote a book about tall tales of the Appalachian Trail, do not write tall tales of the Appalachian Trail II. Think about something like mythical creatures of the Appalachian Trail.

Another way to consider what might work is to look at individual chapters from your book. Was there one chapter that was particularly large, or difficult for people to understand? Was there one chapter that people always ask questions about? Perhaps the topic of this chapter alone could make a book.

Also, when considering the title of a potential second book, think about the title of the first one as well. Try to build on it, if the books are related. Think in terms of a series for all of your books if the books are to have long-term staying power.

Another option is revising your current book. Some topics lend themselves to frequent updates, others do not. If your book is the type that needs frequent revision to stay current, there are a lot of incentives to release new versions. The number one reason is that when your book says second or third or fourth edition (hopefully prominently displayed on the cover), it broadcasts success to the reader. It says that the book was worthwhile to revise and reissue. The second reason is that it helps reduce your vulnerability to the used book market. Used books, especially through amazon.com, have started to degrade sales and therefore the author's royalties.

By issuing new editions, it will make the readers want the new updated version, and not the older, out-of-date, used version. One important note: if you do issue a new edition, make sure it is substantively revised, and not just cosmetically tweaked. If readers buy both editions and find them virtually identical, they will feel duped and will not buy books with your name again.

The best way to start to work on revising your book is to keep a copy or a file handy when you speak. Any comments or observations about what is missing or what sections are too wordy? Note it in the file. Questions arise from the audience about a topic not covered? They must have wanted it to be in the book; add it next time. Did a customer email you compliments about it? Ask him or her what he or she would like to see added in future editions. Customers will be honored by the request. Every time you are talking to someone who read the book, think of the next edition.

Happily Ever After

Some people will read this book and execute each step as they read it. Hopefully, your book is selling. Sales are as good as you hoped, or better. You have given talks and book signings. You have a second idea in the works. Your publisher is interested in the topic and wants to hear more.

If, however, you read through the whole book to understand the process and have done none of the steps yet (which is the most likely scenario), now it is time to get going. You have within you what is necessary. Most of what you needed you had before you even started this book. It takes determination, commitment, and desire.

I started the book by telling you 81% of everyone in the United States felt they could write a book. As I mentioned, that would be over 200 million books. However, there are about 200,000 new books published each year. That is a big gap. Do not dream and then not act on your dream.

You truly can write, publish, and sell your book. Now is the time to start. I hope to buy a copy of your book someday, or perhaps you can send me an autographed one.

Bibliography

Applebaum, Judith. *How to Get Happily Published*, 5th ed. New York: Harpers Resource Book, 1998.

Bailee, Dehanna. *The ABC's of POD: A Beginner's Guide to Fee-Based Print-on-Demand Publishing*. Huntersville, NC: Blue Leaf Publications, 2005.

Blanco, Jodee. *The Complete Guide to Book Publicity*, 2nd ed. New York: Allworth Press, 2004.

Bly, Robert W. *The Copywriter's Handbook: A Step-by-Step Guide to Writing That Sells*. New York: Henry Holt, 1985.

Boice, Robert. *Professors as Writers: A Self-Help Guide to Productive Writing*. Stillwater, OK: New Forums Press, Inc, 1990.

Bolton, Lesley. *The Everything Guide to Writing Children's Books: From Cultivating an Idea to Finding the Right Publisher—All You Need to Launch a Successful Career*. Avon, MA: Adams Media Corporation, 2003.

Bykofsky, Sheree, and Jennifer Sander. *The Complete Idiot's Guide to Getting Published*. New York: Alpha Books, 2003.

Cole, David. *The Complete Guide to Book Marketing*, rev. ed. New York: Allworth Press, 2003.

Condrill, Jo, and John B. Slack. *From Book Signing to Best Seller: An Insider's Guide to Conducting a Successful Low-Cost Book Signing Tour*. Beverly Hills, CA: Goal Minds, 2001.

Frey, James. *How to Write a Damn Good Novel*. New York: St. Martin's Press, 1987.

Harnish, John F. *Everything You Always Wanted to Know About POD Publishing But Didn't Know Who To Ask*. Haverford, PA: Infinity Publishing, 2002.

Herman, Jeff. *Jeff Herman's Guide to Book Publishers, Editors, and Literary Agents, 2005*. Wauesha, WI: Writer, Incorporated, 2004.

Herman, Jeff, and Deborah Adams. *Write the Perfect Book Proposal: 10 Proposals That Sold and Why*. New York: John Wiley & Sons, 1993.

Jassin, Lloyd, and Steve Shecter. *The Copyright Permission and Libel Handbook*. New York: John Wiley & Sons, 1998.

Kiefer, Marie. *Book Publishing Resource Guide*, 5th ed. Fairfield, IA: Ad-Lib Publications, 1996.

Kirsch, Jonathan. *Kirsch's Guide to the Book Contract*. Los Angeles, CA: Acrobat Books, 1999.

Kirsch, Jonathan. *Kirsch's Handbook of Publishing Law*. Los Angeles, CA: Acrobat Books, 1995.

Kremer, John. *1001 Ways to Market Your Book*. 5th ed. Fairfield, IA: Open Horizons, 2000.

Lamott, Anne. *Bird to Bird: Some Instructions on Writing and Life*. New York: Anchor Books, 1994.

Larsen, Michael. *How to Write a Book Proposal*. Cincinnati, OH: Writer's Digest Books, 1997.

Larsen, Michael. *Literary Agents: What They Do, How They Do It, and How to Find and Work with the Right One for You, Revised and Expanded*. New York: John Wiley & Sons, 1996.

Levine, Mark L. *Negotiating a Book Contract*. Wakefield, RI: Moyer Bell, 1988.

Levinson, Jay Conrad, Rick Frishman, Rick, and Michael Larsen. *Guerrilla Marketing for Writers*. Cincinnati, OH: Writer's Digest Books, 2001.

Literary Market Place 2005. Medford, NJ: Information Today, Inc., 2005.

Lyons, Elizabeth. *Nonfiction Book Proposals Anybody Can Write: How to Get a Contract and an Advance Before Writing Your Book*. Portland, OR: Blue Heron Press, 1995.

Page, Susan. *The Shortest Distance Between You and a Published Book: 20 Steps to Success*. New York: Broadway Books, 1997.

Poynter, Dan. *The Self-Publishing Manual*, 14th ed. Santa Barbara, CA: Para Publishing, 2003.

Rose, M. J., and Angela Adair-Hoy. *How to Publish and Promote Online*. New York: St. Martin's Griffin, 2001.

Ross, Marilyn, and Tom Ross. *Jump Start Your Book Sales: A Money-Making Guide for Authors, Independent Publishers and Small Presses*. Buena Vista, CO: Communication Creativity, 1999.

Ross, Tom, and Marilyn Ross. *The Complete Guide to Self-Publishing*, 4th ed. Cincinnati, OH: Writer's Digest Books. 2002.

Rubie, Peter. *The Everything Get Published Book*. Avon, MA: Adams Media Corporation, 2000.

Stine, Jean Marie. *Writing Successful Self-Help & How-To Books: An Insider's Guide to Everything You Need to Know*. New York: John Wiley & Sons, 1997.

Strunk, William, and E. B. White. *The Elements of Style*. New York, NY: Pearson Higher Education, 1997.

Thomas, Suzanne P. *Make Money Self-Publishing*. Boulder, CO: Gemstone House Publishing, 2001.

University of Chicago Press Staff. *The Chicago Manual of Style*, 15th ed. Chicago, IL: University of Chicago, 2003.

Woll, Thomas. *Selling Subsidiary Rights: An Insider's Guide*. Tucson, AZ: Fisher Books, 2000.

Zackheim, Sarah Parsons. *Getting Your Book Published for Dummies*. Foster City, CA: IDG Books, 2000.

Appendix

Publishing Resources

Agent Resources

Agent Query .... www.agentquery.com

Agent Research & Evaluation .... www.agentresearch.com

Association of Authors' Representatives .... www.aar-online.org

Authorlink.. www.authorlink.com

Everyone Who's Anyone
in Adult Trade Publishing.............. www.everyonewhosanyone.com

First Writer .... www.firstwriter.com

Associations or Trade Groups

American Book Producers Association .... www.abpaonline.org

American Booksellers Association .... www.bookweb.org

American Library Association .... www.ala.org
American Screenwriters Association .... www.goasa.com
Association of American Publishers .... www.publishers.org
Authors Guild .... www.authorsguild.org
Friends of Libraries USA .... www.folusa.org
National Writers Union .... www.nwu.org
PMA, the Independent Book
Publishers Association .... www.pma-online.org
Public Relations Society of America............................... www.prsa.org
Small Press Center .... www.smallpress.org
Small Publishers Association
of North America .... www.spannet.org

Book Marketing Resources

All You Can Read .... www.allyoucanread.com
Authors and Experts .... www.authorsandexperts.com
Blogsearchengine .... www.blogsearchengine.com
Blogwise .... www.blogwise.com
Book Announcements .... www.bookannouncements.com
Book-Clubs-Resource .... www.book-clubs-resource.com
Book Connector .... www.bookconnector.com
Book Marketing.. www.bookmarket.com
Bookpage .... www.bookpage.com
Experts... www.experts.com
Ezine Directory .... www.ezine-dir.com
Guest Finder .... www.guestfinder.com

Jenkins Group .... www.bookpublishing.com
Midwest Book Review .... www.midwestbookreview.com
News Buzz... www.newsbuzz.com
PubLounge .... www.publounge.com
Radio-TV Interview Report .... www.rtir.com
Speak and Grow Rich .... www.speakandgrowrich.com
Toastmasters .... www.toastmasters.org
vBulletin/ Discussion Forum .... www.vbulletin.com/links.php
Zinester .... www.zinester.com

General Publishing Resources

BookWire .... www.bookwire.com
Library of Congress .... www.loc.gov
Literary Market Place .... www.literarymarketplace.com
Publishing Game .... www.publishinggame.com
Publishing Law Center .... www.publaw.com
Publishers Lunch/Marketplace .... www.publishersmarketplace.com

On-Line Bookstores

Alibris .... www.alibris.com
Amazon .... www.amazon.com
Barnes & Noble .... www.bn.com
Books-A-Million .... www.booksamillion.com
Powell's Books.. www.powells.com

Plus a listing of
independent bookstores ....www.bookweb.org/bookstores

Publishing and Writing References or Publications

Creativity for Life ....www.creativityforlife.com
Independent Publisher ....www.independentpublisher.com
Publish L Listserve ....www.publish-L.com
Publisher's Forum Listserve ....www.pub-forum.net
Publishers Weekly ....www.publishersweekly.com
Publishing Trends ....www.publishingtrends.com
Writer Magazine ....www.writermag.com
Writers Break ....www.writersbreak.com
Writer's Digest ....www.writersdigest.com
Writers Market ....www.writersmarket.com
Writers-Publish ....www.writers-publish.com
Writing-World ....www.writing-world.com

Publishing Services and Print-on-demand Services

AuthorHouse ....www.authorhouse.com
Fultus Corporation...www.fultus.com
Infinity Publishing.....................................www.infinitypublishing.com
Instant Publisher...www.instantpublisher.com
iUniverse ....www.iuniverse.com

Llumina Press .... www.llumina.com
Trafford Publishing .... www.trafford.com
Xlibris .... www.xlibris.com

Search Engines

Excite .... www.excite.com
Google .... www.google.com
MSN Search .... search.msn.com
Yahoo .... www.yahoo.com

Self-Publishing Resources

Go Publish Yourself .... www.go-publish-yourself.com
Para Publishing .... www.parapub.com

Index

About the Author

John Bond's life has revolved around books, reading, and publishing; he has worked for nearly 20 years in publishing. He has worked for a publisher in New Jersey that specializes in medical information, SLACK Incorporated. He started as an Editor, and eventually became the Vice President and Publisher for the company's Book Division.

In his career, he has published over 400 projects, including books, CD-ROMs, videotapes, posters, study cards, and DVDs. Some of these projects were student textbooks, manuals, workbooks, dictionaries, monographs, and instructor's manuals.

He has helped formulate and create several web sites that provide information to health care providers. He has worked with such publishers as Random House, Henry Holt, McGraw Hill, Doubleday, and Thomson International on special projects or on distribution arrangements.

He is a proud member of the Publisher's Marketing Association, the Small Publishers of North America, and the American Medical Publishers Association. He has given presentations at meetings involving emerging topics related to publishing.

Prior to his work in publishing, he earned a degree in education and worked as a librarian for five years.

An avid reader and book collector, he first developed an interest in books at auctions as a child (pre-eBay days) when his family bought 10 boxes of books for $1.00. The joy of looking through those boxes for something unique led him to where he is today.

He lives in southern New Jersey with his wife Theresa and their three boys, Andrew, Kevin, and Peter.

Let Me Know What You Think

- Have a comment about the book?
- Want to give a compliment?
- Register a complaint?
- Want to suggest a book or web site to add to the list of Publishing Resources or Bibliography?
- Have a question?

You can email me at questions@riverwindspublishing.com. I will also keep you up to date with new information in publishing.

Thanks in advance for your comments and questions.

John Bond